I CAN
READ
YOUR
FACE

I CAN READ YOUR FACE

LAURA ROSETREE

ILLUSTRATIONS BY PAULA STONE

A DELL TRADE PAPERBACK

A DELL TRADE PAPERBACK
Published by
Dell Publishing
a division of
Bantam Doubleday Dell Publishing Group, Inc.
666 Fifth Avenue
New York, New York 10103

First edition published as *I CAN READ YOUR FACE*
by AHA! Experiences

Face Reading Secrets™ is a term used by Laura Rosetree for her
unique method of facial analysis.

ISBN: 0-440-50309-4

Printed in the United States of America
Published simultaneously in Canada
Design by Snap Haus Graphics

January 1991

10 9 8 7 6 5 4 3 2 1

RRC

DEDICATION

We Americans agree we'd prefer a kinder, gentler nation. But did you ever notice how we treat each other?

So often we glance at a stranger, make a judgment, and move on. "Do I like her expression?" "Is he attractive?"

We decide on that all-important first impression. Usually, it's negative.

That's about as kind as a slap in the face!

Well, I have found a way to go beyond appearances, so I can look at others in the way I wish they would see me . . . as a unique individual who is worth knowing.

The Face Reading Secrets clue me in—in depth, in detail. Each person becomes a fascinating mixture of strengths and challenges. Even if studiously hidden, all these traits can be read. Outer face reveals inner person, once you know where to look.

Because I have cracked this code, every face tells me its secrets. Reader, you can learn to find them too. Don't settle for anything less.

Reading the secrets gives you a practical edge, for more success whenever you deal with people. Personally, I'm grateful for that. But I'm even more grateful to Face Reading Secrets for opening me up emotionally, to reach a level of unconditional love for people that I never felt before. This includes love for myself and how I look.

I dedicate this book to you, in that spirit of gratitude.

ACKNOWLEDGMENTS

Each of the following people helped me to develop or present the knowledge of Face Reading Secrets. The list is part history of ideas, part life story, part situational gratitude. Since the reasons for my acknowledgments are numerous, sometimes complicated, and invariably mushy, the names alone will be written. You may recognize a few.

THANK YOU. Lillian, Paula Stone, Anne Edelstein, Pat Capon, Jody Rein, Josquin Des Pres, Amy Patton, Debra Leopold, Harold Levin, Jeffrey Chappell, Mick and Martha Collins, Raphael, Sue and Alex Kramer, C. S. Lewis, Rhoda Weber, Ernie Rosenbaum, Lailan Young, Merlin, Nancy Amidei, Art Boucher, Christina Haslinger, Elaine Cooperman, Virginia Woolf, Jenny Rouse, Don Anderson, Gloria Ross, Michaele and Chris Kapilla, Dick Katz, Allen Grossman, Richard Onorato, Karl Mannheim, Monica Lacrouts, Susan Kingsley-Rowe, Elliot Carlson, The Beatles, Debra Sue Poneman, Joanna Lester, Aldous Huxley, David Rothleder, Rosa Linares, Lynda Rosenberg, Hermann Hesse, Howard Christopher Moss, Andrea Myers, Joanne Brandt, William Shakespeare, Hannah Sard, John Kremer, Don Zuckerman, Gerard Manley Hopkins; most of the famous people whose faces are used as examples, the face reader at MENSA who got me started, and, especially, Mitch Weber.

CONTENTS

INTRODUCTION TO FACE READING SECRETS

What's the first thing *you* look for when you meet a stranger?

If you are like most people, you watch the eyes. Your deductions may be so on target that you figure you're already reading faces. But if this is all you do, you're missing the hidden essentials.

Many sets of information are available to us as observers. Facial expression is one set, as are speech and action. Body language (emblematic gestures and other nonverbal communication) also gives useful clues to understanding.

Probably the most frequently used set of information we watch for is pure demographics. Sex, race, age, and even socioeconomic status show on the surface. You're probably an expert at this form of face watching.

Another set of information is physical attractiveness.

If a face isn't good-looking by our standards or we don't like the expression, if we are prejudiced against race or age, if we don't like the stranger's mood (as we interpret it), we could throw a perfectly good human being in the trash. Unwittingly, we deprive ourselves of countless relationships that could enrich our personal or professional lives.

Judging by appearances also makes it easier for others to fool us.

Say, for example, you meet Chloe at a singles mixer. Looking at her eyes, you can tell she is fascinated by you. She seems meek and mild, easy to dominate. In fact, Chloe just lost her boyfriend because she was bossy and controlling. All her past relationships with men showed the same pattern.

But now Chloe plans to reform. Sort of. She hasn't done significant emotional or spiritual work to change inside; she simply decides on a superficial level that now she's going to be just the opposite from before.

She may or may not be fooling herself. She definitely wants to fool you.

So she comes across meek and mild, acting in her role of The New, Improved Chloe. Consequently, her expression, body language, speech, and actions all proclaim it.

Only by reading her face could you see that her long-term character trait is just the opposite.

Face reading involves looking at the physical traits in a face, such as ears and eyebrows, to get a picture of inner character. It works like a form of literacy. Once you learn your ABC's, you can read any face in the world.

In China, this study of physiognomy is as traditional as acupuncture. It is called *Siang Mien* (pronounced SEE-ahng MEE-un), meaning "investigating spirit."

In Western culture, the tradition goes back to Plato and Aristotle. More recently, facial observation has been used for generations by homeopathic physicians (practitioners of an alternative form of medicine that was common in America before the world wars and still has a following today).

I began studying face reading in 1976, when my own face was read, with startling accuracy, by a practitioner of Siang Mien. For a decade, I read everything on Siang Mien I could find.

During this research I got my feelings hurt pretty regularly. Siang Mien is full of judgmental statements about people who do not have "the best" features. When facial traits you can't help carry names like "fox eyes" and "chicken eyes," is it any wonder that Siang Mien isn't everyone's favorite hobby?

Nevertheless, I agreed with the premise of Siang Mien that facial features reveal character. Some of the specific interpretations of facial traits also rang true. However, I threw away the parts I considered nasty and judgmental, which was most of it.

To add more knowledge, I drew on my own intuition. For years I have worked as a spiritual counselor and minister of the Universal Life Church. Clients say my perceptions help to change their lives for the better.

Whatever the ultimate explanation of my discovery, all I know for sure is how it happened: I had the desire to develop a better system of face reading. I plugged into my intuition, let go, and got zapped with new ideas that felt true. By 1986 I had put together the system of Face Reading Secrets. I test it by getting direct feedback from the people whose faces I read.

This discovery is perfect for the 1990s, because it transposes the ancient wisdom of Siang Mien to meet the needs of Americans today.

AN AMAZING TOOL
FOR COMMUNICATION

- Someone is about to offer you a job. During the interview your potential boss has emphasized the importance of carrying projects through to completion. *Wouldn't you like to know* whether she does this herself? Maybe she's expecting you to handle all the details, for you and for her.
- You are selling shoes to a man who happens to be in a grouchy mood. What good does it do to tell he is grouchy? *Wouldn't you like to know* the kind of small talk you can use to change his mood?
- You're at a party, nonchalantly screening a potential date. Like you, he says he's interested in books and jogging. But wouldn't you like to know *how* interested? Don't take it for granted that his interest in exercise is like yours, just because it sounds the same. Maybe jogging is his burning passion, while for you it's mostly a way to cool down a seething, superintellectual brain.

If communication between people were just a matter of information, we could go beyond computer dates and have computer relationships. You and your partner would tap into each other's databases and, quicker than you can say Pac-Man, be set for life.

Really, *how* we communicate is just as important as *what* we communicate. We need to fine tune what we have to say according to how the listener hears. Face Reading Secrets helps, because it makes you aware of personal style.

And this inside information can come to you in seconds, before anyone utters a word. You don't have to say: "Let's skip the stuff about the weather. Tell me about your drive for power, your habits with money, and how fast you make decisions."

Few people could answer such questions objectively, even if they wanted to. Fortunately, you can read the Secrets without having to ask. All it takes is one good look. So this could be the most important tool you ever receive to master social situations. You will see other people, and yourself, so much more clearly.

READING YOUR OWN FACE

The most important face for you to learn to read is your own. Sure, you may already know plenty about your personal style. What you don't know is how it shows in your face.

Think back to your childhood and those seemingly endless teenage years, critical times for shaping your subconscious self-image. Did kids ever make fun of your nose or your chin? The humiliation lingers. According to a survey in *Psychology Today*, 30 million Americans are ashamed of their chins, and 60 million hate their noses.

Even professional models find fault with their faces. That's how society trains us. The prevalence of eating disorders in our country, the billion-dollar cosmetics industry, the growing popularity of plastic surgery, document the sad truth: Too few of us are in love with how we look.

In my work, I often hear stories from folks who wish they looked different, whose features have been given labels like "pug nose" and "Dumbo ears."

In fact, the very features people are most ashamed of can be related to exceptional talents. Even a so-called ordinary-looking face reveals a unique set of talents and abilities, once you know how to read it.

Just on a physical level, Face Reading Secrets may teach you to recognize facial traits for the first time. When I give my hour-long face sessions, it is rare for me *not* to find at least one trait my client never noticed before. What really delights me, though, is to see people leave those sessions glowing with a new awareness that: *My face is perfect, just the way it is, because it perfectly expresses who I am inside.*

You, too, will see your face differently once you understand its inner significance. Contrary to the fears you may have, based on harsh experiences of being judged by others, Face Reading Secrets will strengthen your self-esteem.

THE SKEPTICS SPEAK

Heredity

"What about heredity?" people have asked. "Your facial traits simply reflect what you picked out of your parents' gene pool."

Different levels of life exist without invalidating each other. Your hand under a microscope looks different from the hand you shake to greet a new friend; both realities are your hand.

Of course heredity is a valid level of life. But each of us still picks one set of genes rather than another. Siblings don't look identical. Even identical twins wind up looking different from each other as they grow up.

Beliefs and interests run in families, too, don't they? Why be surprised if people who think alike also look alike?

Incidentally, did you ever notice how devoted spouses come to resemble each other? Faces change more than most folks realize.

Race

Some individuals have criticized my work, claiming it contributes to prejudice.

I can only comment that such a criticism in itself reflects prejudice. After all, the premise of this criticism is "You are going to read all blacks [or Chinese or Jews or Italians, etc.] alike because they look the same."

Do all the members of ethnic groups look the same? Of

course not. Only when vision is shadowed by stereotypes do people assume others look interchangeable.

Face Reading secrets helps us notice the unique qualities of people, improving our recognition of the individualistic shapes, angles, and proportions in faces of every ethnicity. My goal is to help people learn to really look at each other, exactly the opposite of the close-minded, perfunctory way of seeing that is so common in America today.

Superficiality

"In next year's election for D.C. mayor, you can study the records of the candidates or you can study their faces."

That's how an article in *The Washingtonian* prefaced an interview where I read the faces of Mayor Marion Barry and Jesse Jackson. I was appalled.

Never would I recommend voting for someone based on looks. Hiring someone based on looks. Or marrying someone based just on looks.

What I do advocate is that you supplement information from the usual sources by reading the Secrets. Take the example of hiring. As a job candidate, you're evaluated on your qualifications. But your character is also judged, during the interview and through checking references. Similarly, as a job seeker, you go after every bit of information you can get on a potential employer.

What would you say if your friend Mr. Smith offered to give you firsthand knowledge about a prospective boss's character? Would you hesitate? Not likely.

Before clinching a business deal, it's smart to find out all you can about the players. You shouldn't have to belong to the old-boy network to do it.

The inside scoop on personality might make the difference between a choice that looks great on the surface and a big mistake.

That's why 85 percent of the businesses in Western Europe rely on handwriting analysis in their hiring procedures.

Face Reading Secrets is easier to learn and fulfills the same purpose.

Cosmetic Surgery

"What if a man gets a nose job? There goes your ability to read his face."

Not so. I've had clients who have had cosmetic surgery. They told me how their faces looked before. Then I told them how I thought their styles had changed.

My assessments were right on the money, every time.

You see, the premise of reading faces is that the facial characteristics you have *right now* reflect your inner qualities *right now*.

Most commonly, our outer physical traits change over time, reflecting the inner changes that occur with growth and age. However, you can also work change from the outside in, through surgery, accidents, eyebrow plucking—whatever. The inner traits will change in a corresponding manner.

Skeptical? Ask someone who has had plastic surgery if his feelings about himself have changed.

"But isn't it cheating if you change the way you were supposed to be?"

I don't take any position about the ethics of cosmetic surgery. However, I do want to emphasize that my system of face reading is holistic. Each part of us reflects the whole. If you change inside or outside, the rest of you will change too.

Fortune-telling

When people raise this objection to my work, I have to laugh. I don't want to tell fortunes any more than most people want to hear them.

Fortune-telling is a prominent feature of Siang Mien, but not of my face reading system.

Do you want to work toward a wonderful future? Create that future by recognizing your greatest strengths as an individual, and play up your strengths. Too many people underuse their talents because they are so busy trying to live up to other people's values and expectations.

Face Reading Secrets can help you identify the strengths of your personal style. Therefore, it *won't* predict your future, but *will* empower you to make your future the best it can be.

C H A P T E R
2

THE RULES

Before you delve into the following chapters, here are a few helpful rules for interpretation.

STRENGTHS, CHALLENGES, AND LIFE LESSONS

An important principle of Face Reading Secrets is that each strength goes with a potential challenge.

Each facial trait indicates a talent or ability related to personal style. Whenever you see that trait, you can be sure the person has that strength.

But the bitter goes with the sweet. Potential challenges accompany each strength. Once someone learns the life lesson associated with that challenge, it disappears. Only the strength remains.

Suppose your ears stick way out from your head. You're sure to have the strength of nonconformity—an independent way of setting your own agenda. You don't wait for others to take the lead.

With ears like that, you may be a great leader. Potentially, though, you may come across like the proverbial bull in a china shop. Is that a challenge for you or not?

The answer depends on whether you stop to check in with others. Do you monitor the effect you are having? If not, you will have a challenge with tact . . . until you master the life lesson of using independence wisely.

Other systems of face reading focus on fault finding. My system reframes faults in terms of strengths, emphasizing personal growth. Often, I've found, the best way to fix what doesn't work is to acknowledge a related aspect of style that does work.

Will it help to berate Fred for being tactless? Don't waste your time! Instead, acknowledge his independence; then he'll find it easier to temper independence with consideration for others.

As a face reader, you are forewarned and thus forearmed against people's shortcomings. Just remember, a challenge isn't a life sentence. It's a potential difficulty that can be overcome. You can't determine challenges by reading a single face trait.

SEE IT STRAIGHT

As you prepare to study your subject's face, make sure she is at a straight angle from you. When you look upward or downward, some physical traits get distorted.

So look on the level, whether you are holding a mirror up to your face or to someone else's.

BE PREPARED FOR SOME NEW IDEAS

You'll be learning to see many facial traits in a new way, so give yourself some time to practice.

A "big nose," for instance, has many aspects to it, not just overall size. Where is it biggest, at the tip, nostrils, or roots? Is it long in proportion to the other features? Wide at the bridge or all the way down?

Each of these traits could make a nose look big, but they mean different things. Unfortunately, most folks register "big nose" and don't stick around to notice exactly where it is big.

Let me reassure you that you don't have to start out being observant to become a skilled face reader. It comes naturally, as you take pleasure in discovering the significance of specific details.

VERY = VERY

Life isn't black and white. Even black-and-white photographs show halftones. It's the same with physical traits. The characteristics you read will vary from one subject to another. So remember this rule when you interpret:

A VERY extreme face trait = a VERY extreme character trait.

When you compare one face to another, you will start to notice *contrasting* characteristics. For example, compare the shapes of Jane's and Fred's noses. Maybe his is straighter while hers is more arched. Once you get the difference between contrasting facial traits, you'll notice that some arched noses are very arched, while others arch only slightly.

Arches go with the need to solve problems creatively. So interpret a *very* arched nose as a *very* strong need to solve problems creatively. For a slightly arched nose, this need is not so compelling.

For any trait, you'll want to decide if it is very big or very small, versus just *somewhat* big or small. Go by the proportions within the face. To see if Fred's nose tip is big, for instance, don't decide by comparing his nose to Jane's. He may have larger features all around. Instead, compare the size of his nose tip to the size of his eyes and lips.

If you judge a facial trait, like nose tip size, to be very *big*, expect the corresponding inner trait of prizing financial security to be extreme—as in the examples noted later of Claude Pepper and Ralph Nader.

Nose tips that are somewhat big mean that the emphasis on saving is less pronounced.

By the same token, the trait of *small* nose tip has significance. If it is *very* tiny the corresponding behavior trait—unconcern with saving money—is *very* pronounced.

See what I mean by VERY = VERY?

At first you may want to comment only on features you can eyeball easily. A clear case of big jaws, for example, reveals that someone has great physical stamina. But as your observation develops, subtle variations will emerge. You'll notice when features are chiseled into sharp clarity versus when they are vaguely defined. This adds depth to your interpretations.

MIXED SIDES

Few faces are truly symmetrical. See for yourself. Look in a mirror. Cover one side of your face with a sheet of white paper. Then cover the other. Two different people!

As you start scrutinizing features you're bound to notice asymmetry more. During all the years that Jimmy Carter was in office as president, did you ever notice that his ears are positioned quite differently? Take a look next time you see his picture—you're not likely to miss it now.

Keep looking at faces and soon you'll notice mismatched nostrils, cheeks and eyebrows of different shapes, and more.

Is asymmetry a goof of nature? No, because every trait on the face is significant. The contrasts add complexity to your face portraits. For instance, how do you interpret when one nostril shows generosity, the other, stinginess?

It's a conflict you should point out in your face reading. Your subject may help you interpret. Was fear of spending a past lesson that has been overcome, so that past and present show on the face? Or is spend-versus-don't-spend a continuing conflict that your subject struggles with day by day?

DEVELOPING YOUR INTUITION

Trust your first reaction when you assess facial traits. To the extent you diverge from scientific measurement, you are using intuition.

Sometimes students ask if my face reading method can be used to develop intuition. The answer is emphatically yes.

Contrary to popular myth, extrasensory perception doesn't usually announce itself in a flashy way. It's beyond the obvious physical senses, hence the term *extra*. In fact, ESP is simply applied intuition, and *intuition* means being taught or guided from within.

So don't wait to see a six-inch pink-and-gold spotlight around your best friend with the word *** A*U*R*A *** lit up and blinking like the neon sign for a cheap motel. You are more likely to feel an aura than see it.

Intuition speaks to us through subtle feelings. Making intuition clearer can be as simple as paying attention to your hunches. Three steps are involved:

1. Choose to listen to your instincts. (All of us get inner guidance constantly. We just don't pay much attention.)

2. Demonstrate your good faith by acting on what you receive. Often this comes down to a choice between your reasoning mind and your feelings. To strengthen intuition, make the choice that feels emotionally right.

3. Give thanks when your intuition pays off. Thank God or yourself—whoever you believe is in charge. The point here is

not politeness. It's just that what we acknowledge tends to grow stronger in our lives. This is a law of consciousness.

In the following chapters you will see how to bridge the material aspects of physical appearances with the inner emotional and spiritual aspects. You would have to work hard *not* to have your intuition improve as you use this knowledge.

A NOT SO MINOR POINT

Is it wise to read everyone's face? Are there cases where it won't be helpful? Yes—for someone under seventeen years of age.

Faces change too much in the early years. Besides, younger people are more impressionable. Let those faces and bodies continue to develop at their own pace before slapping labels on them.

If you're younger, I recommend that you don't try to read your own face but look for Face Reading Secrets in others. You can never start too early.

C H A P T E R
3

EYEBROWS

Ever wish you could open up people's brains to watch how they think? Learn to read eyebrows. It's a lot less messy.

To read an eyebrow, begin with the start-up hairs (nearest the nose) and follow the brow pattern out to the end. Different traits within the eyebrow will clue you in to different aspects of your subject's thinking patterns.

THICKNESS

EVEN brows show about the same thickness, or distribution of hair, from startup to end. This is rarer than you would expect.

An **even**-browed person's thought process flows smoothly. He gets an idea, follows it through, and works out all the related details. This gift might be taken for granted by these people, but shouldn't be. It's definitely an advantage for work projects.

In fact, the only potential challenge with this eyebrow trait is *lack of tolerance for the rest of humanity's* ability with details. How can others get so sloppy? How can they get so bogged down?

VERY THICK, even eyebrows are the mark of unusually powerful thinking. You'll observe them on the faces of many leaders.

The power may be political, as in the case of Israeli prime minister Golda Meir. Social causes may be at stake, as with the generous brows of Roy Wilkins, executive secretary of the National Association for the Advancement of Colored People. The power may be expressed gently, as in the work of the Reverend Fred Rogers, known to millions of children as "Mister Rogers."

STARTER brows come on strong at the start, then they wimp out. The later part may even show gaps with no hair at all.

The more contrasting the thickness between start and end, the greater the challenge a person faces in following through with the practical details of daily life.

This can be read very specifically. A person whose brows thin out halfway through typically loses interest halfway through projects. If the brows thin out three quarters of the way through then most of the job gets done before dealing with the details feels like a nuisance.

Brows that fade out a quarter of the way through reflect major potential challenge with follow-through.

On the positive side, people with **starter** brows generate more new creative ideas than the other eyebrow types. Why do these folks lose interest in details before completing a project? Because so many other ideas for new projects have rushed in. Maybe the folks with these visionary brows aren't the best to depend on for details, but turn to them when you need a brilliant new brainstorm.

Inventor Thomas Edison had **starter** eyebrows, as did Florence Nightingale and Louis Pasteur.

Matthew Henson's eyebrows may have given him the start-up power to put on all that cold weather gear and get going on his polar explorations.

Thickness

| Even | Starter | Ender |

Poet Rainer Maria Rilke had starter brows; so did an even more mystical poet, Walt Whitman. His face was dominated by abundant brows, with long hairs growing in an upward direction, placed high above his eyes.

Strong starters may have to make a concerned effort to follow through. They might also consider collaborating with the folks who excel at details. . . .

ENDER eyebrows are the ones that broaden out as they get going. Their owners have a talent for following through loose ends, no matter how numerous (or insignificant) they may be. Read each of those extra hairs as a detail masterfully handled.

Strong-at-the-finish eyebrows reveal a potential challenge too. These people do a great job once they get going. The trick is to get going.

Inertia is especially apt to be a problem if the brows start off looking skimpy. Now, I'm not talking about everyday procrastination here, which can strike all eyebrow types, for a variety of reasons. This inertia is a deep-down dread of beginning.

Perhaps it's because these perfectionists know what they're in for, once they begin. What they start, they finish, and finish magnificently. The quick and dirty jobs are not for them—they go for methodical and tidy, very tidy.

Yet, provided that the problem of inertia is overcome, these people can be dynamite. Almost literally. Siang Mien notes that people with such eyebrows make excellent soldiers—just the extra ammunition to have around during a long-drawn-out battle.

(This holds especially true if the eyebrows are set in a face that is shaped like a diamond and has protruding cheekbones with hollows beneath them.)

Completion eyebrows can be helpful in more peaceful occupations as well. Witness the craftsmanship of cellist Yo-Yo Ma and Kenzo Tange, the dean of contemporary Japanese architecture.

The great Russian film director Sergei Paradzhanov has hired an incredibly large cast of extras—right on his face. The crowd of hairs swells to a mob as it parades across his forehead. In the symbolism of face reading, that means his thinking welcomes details—and plenty of them. It follows that his films are concerned with the lives of Soviet ethnic minorities, people whose live are the "details" of Russian society.

CONTRADICTORY HAIRS AND OTHER UNUSUAL EYEBROW BEHAVIOR

Details are, indeed, the specialty of the person whose eyebrows end up lavishly. But will all those details help or hinder? For a clue, pay attention to the direction of the hairs.

If the hairs grow in the same direction, all is well. But should some hairs grow downward and tangle up, beware of a potential challenge: **CONTRADICTORY HAIRS.**

People who wear these brows can suffer from repeated challenges due to contradictory thought patterns. And chances are that folks with conflict over *thoughts* will attract conflict with *people*—family members, business associates, and others.

Some eyebrow hairs are **SCATTERED**, with hairs that grow out of line. That reflects scattered ideas and represents a challenge of a different sort.

For people with either scattered or contradictory thinking, meditation could be indispensable for releasing inner stress.

Do you know anyone whose **EYEBROW ROOTS** show? You know, the Brooke Shields look. At the part of the eyebrow closest to the nose, a clump of hairs grow straight up rather than across the forehead. Perhaps most eyebrows start this way, but rarely do they show these hairs growing en masse, as a noticeable clump.

What's so great about these naked, straggly beginnings of eyebrows? Why have they become so popular in our culture that you can see cover girls openly flaunting their roots? These hairs symbolize the early stages of thought development. Visible hairs symbolize that their owner has conscious access to thoughts and feelings at an earlier stage of development than most people. When a subject with visible roots embarks on a new project, he will anticipate potential problems right from the start. This awareness can result in the ability to nip problems in the bud, but may also contribute to habits of nagging worry.

Songwriter James Taylor reveals such awareness in many of his lyrics, and his eyebrows confirm it.

As for eyebrows that grow straight across the forehead to give the **UNIBROW** look, read your subject as an intense thinker. Typically, the mind doesn't turn off. Insomnia can be a problem.

Actually, this is the one facial trait that I recommend alter-

Unusual eyebrow features

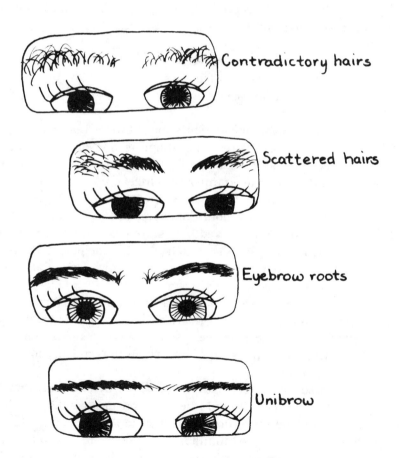

Contradictory hairs

Scattered hairs

Eyebrow roots

Unibrow

ing. Invite your subject with **unibrows** to tweeze, try electrolysis, or otherwise banish those hairs directly over the nose.

Facial and behavioral traits do go together. So calming down nonstop brows may help these intense people to relax.

MENTAL SPECTACLES

Eyebrow shape represents framework for vision. It comes in three models:

- Curved for people-oriented
- Straight for idea-oriented
- Angled for control-oriented

CURVED brows mean your subject frames reality mostly in terms of people. Thus, this shape is one of several facial tip-offs for emotional warmth (others are round chins, full lips, and large or deep inner ear-circles).

The intensity of a subject's involvement with people is proportional to the amount of curve.

Owners of VERY **curved** brows are easily hurt in relationships since they care so much about what people think of them. Siang Mien observes that such brows, when also very thin, denote passion.

This makes sense, since ultra-thin brows, on folks of any eyebrow shape, denote a relatively one-track mind. Put that together with deep concern about other people's opinions and whammo! that's potential dynamite—and if people get lucky, passion.

A person with **STRAIGHT** eyebrows, by contrast, usually focuses on ideas. It could be devotion to a cause, intensity about putting tasks first, or a "passion" for logic—as in the case of *Star Trek*'s inimitable Mr. Spock. In real life, actor Leonard Nimoy's brows are curved. Three cheers for the

Shape

Curved

Straight

Angled

makeup artist who gave him the perfect Vulcan-logical, straight-eyebrow shape.

ANGLED eyebrows can hinge either straight or curved brow shapes together. What sets them apart is the fact that an angle is formed. Sometimes this shape shows because the hair flow changes direction; other times triangles of extra hair form the angle. The fuller the hair and the deeper the angle, the more prominent the character trait. (Remember VERY = VERY.)

People with angled brows do not get as involved in social situations as do the folks who focus on people or concepts. Part of them stands back, evaluating and directing situations with a view to meeting their needs. (Other people do this, too, but not so consciously.)

Managers, social workers, politicians, and movie directors are some of the roles in society where this framework for vision can be used constructively. But the profession where we Americans seem to value angled brows most is in TV journalism. Take a good look at your favorite news show and you're likely to find that the heavy hitter on the team is a man with at least one VERY **angled** eyebrow.

I guess we like having the Sam Donaldson, Edwin Newman types because folks with the very angled brows can be confrontational. They revel in taking charge, interrupting, and otherwise putting their stamp on an interview.

In any walk of life, too much controlling can be interpreted by others as manipulation, even coercion. That's the challenge with the leadership perspective of **angled** eyebrows.

You'll find more examples of angled, straight, and curved brow shapes in the chapter on chins, since brows and chin shapes are related in an interesting way.

One final point to note is that occasionally your subjects will have a second, hidden eyebrow shape. So watch your subject's eyebrows while you do a reading.

When she laughs or talks, does she raise her eyebrows? Lo and behold, straight brows can turn into curves or angles.

This gives you insight into a deeper way your subject sees things. For instance, her perspective may come from ideas most of the time, but when she relaxes and laughs, she sees life in terms of people.

HIGHBROW OR LOWBROW— NO CONTEST

When you look for Face Reading Secrets, the terms *highbrow* and *lowbrow* don't carry their usual meaning. Ordinarily these terms are a cultural label: the Bach-playing violinist in contrast to the bluegrass fiddler, highbrow versus lowbrow.

Well, in terms of reading faces, the distance between brows and eyes tells you more about patience than music-listening habits.

Most of us are **MIDDLEBROWS. HIGHBROWS** signal someone with unusual patience to work out ideas completely, even if it takes a long time.

Remember the previously mentioned **highbrows** of Walt Whitman? He showed monumental patience as he published edition after edition of his *Leaves of Grass*.

LOWBROWS signal a different tempo: the need to express ideas spontaneously. That is when they are in their power, while the highbrows benefit from planning before they speak.

A tip for advanced readers going back over this book: Brow height isn't the easiest trait to read. For the best results, interpret this in conjunction with the cheekbone set (power to follow through in short or long time-span) and length of nose (for preferred style with timing work projects).

Highbrows go comfortably with broad cheeks and a long nose. Lowbrows are a comfortable combination with close-set, prominent cheeks and a short nose. If all three traits fit together, your subject has an especially powerful style of inner timing.

Distance from eyes

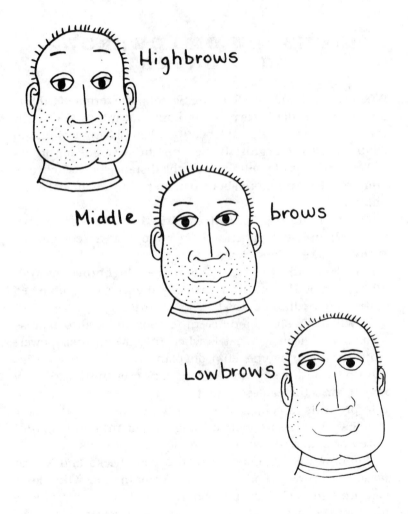

Highbrows

Middle brows

Lowbrows

One example of highbrows where cheeks and nose lend support was the face of Dr. An Wang. The founder of Wang Laboratories, Dr. Wang patiently strategized to establish a $3 billion computer empire.

The contrasting **lowbrow** style is exemplified by Merv Griffin, who got his $300 million fortune rolling as a talk show host. Griffin's brows are so low they practically fall into his eyes. In fact, I've never seen a TV or radio talk show host with **highbrows.**

Controversial Geraldo Rivera has described the advantage of **lowbrows** for reporting: "I just try to react and put it on the air." These words summarize this style at its best— immediacy, personal involvement, and expressivenenss.

Next, let's turn to one of the most revealing—yet underrated— parts of the face.

C H A P T E R

4

EARS

When was the last time you looked a stranger squarely in the ears?

Chances are, after this chapter you will be staring at ears considerably more often. For ears are a marvelous source of Face Reading Secrets.

A SENSE FOR SURPRISE

Hearing may be the most vital of all five senses for bringing us information. For one thing, we think in words mostly, rather than in pictures or fragrances. Consider your every-day experience and you may be struck by how much you depend on listening.

Seeing may convey information faster (as in the proverbial picture worth a thousand words). Yet vision has a curious limitation in terms of how we use it. We must choose what we see by directing our gaze. By contrast, ears pick up sound willy-nilly, taking us by surprise more often than vision.

Ears have a unique way of stretching our knowledge into the unexpected realms. We see what we're willing to look at, while a good listener is constantly taken by surprise.

So ears reveal unconscious patterns of learning, a subject's instinctive style of taking in information. By contrast, eyes show how people learn by consciously paying attention.

SIZE OF LISTENING

The first secret that ears reveal is that, in general, ear size parallels listening ability. **BIG** ears go with a great capacity for listening to others. **SMALL** ears go with less receptivity. Remember, **VERY** = **VERY**.

Though **large**-eared folks make excellent listeners, that doesn't mean folks with the **small** ears are uninterested in others. Often, those with **small** ears have large eyes, suggesting an inner preference for being consciously in control when learning about others. They will be very observant—when they choose to be.

The **large**-eared people are often deluged with input, like it or not, and this overload can represent a challenge.

Sometimes you will find a subject who is so sensitive to people's words that it's fortunate she has **small** ears. She deals so thoroughly with every bit of information that comes in, thank goodness she doesn't take in as much as somebody with larger ears!

LEARNING SPEED

The position of ears clues you in to your subject's learning rate. Usually ears are positioned between the highest part of the eyebrows and the bottom of the nose. Most people have ears placed in this middle region.

Take a good look, though, and you will be surprised. Ear positioning can vary a great deal. Plenty of folks carry their

Position

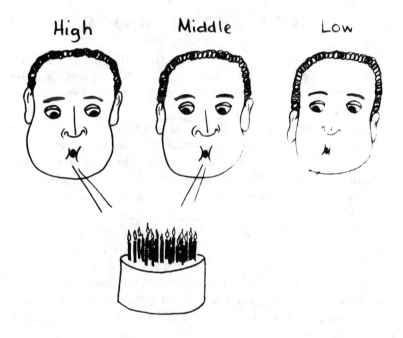

High   Middle   Low

earlobes drooping down below their noses, while others' ear tops are hoisted high, peeking up above their brows.

HIGH EARS, positioned with tops above eyebrows, indicate quicker-than-average processing of information.

Such people learn quickly and make decisions fast. That ability certainly comes in handy for ace jockey Eddie Arcaro.

Another thing—they often think and write fast, as in the case of prolific author Anthony Burgess.

High-placed ears belong to the legendary computer entrepreneur Steve Jobs, as to many who are comfortable working at the rapid pace of computer software design.

Dr. Charles Drew, pioneer in preservation and storage of blood, had high ears and large fangs (just kidding about the fangs). Other innovative high-eared types are geneticist James Watson, town planner Sir Patrick Geddes, and composer Edgard Varèse.

A man with the highest-placed ears I've ever seen caught my attention once at a party. He laughed when I commented on his quick-learner ears.

"Well," he said, "I do speak eighteen languages."

THE POLITICAL WISDOM OF LOW EARS

LOW EARS, with lobes showing beneath the nose, are the tip-off for a slow-but-steady learner. Please understand, in this case *slow* refers to speed, not lack of intelligence. Some of these guys and gals are super smart. Remember, what we're talking about here is personal style of using intelligence.

Brilliant or mediocre, *low-eared* folks process information with a slow thoroughness that can infuriate others. And if you want to infuriate them back . . . just insist on a snap decision.

Low-eared people have enough ego strength to make deliberate, comprehensive decisions. You may notice them weighing many factors before expressing an opinion. They keep on listening long after others have stopped.

As you **high-eared** readers may have guessed by now, many astute political survivors come equipped with low-placed ears, including presidents Bush and Reagan.

A deliberate style is strategically advantageous for politicians. It helps them avoid the challenge of high-eared people: impulsive decisions, based on insufficient information. The high ears want to get closure; the low ears want to get it right. We need both styles to keep society moving.

This extra built-in reaction time has given many low-eared people a chance to develop an unusual perspective on society.

Low-eared historian Edward Gibbon had the patience to put together his masterpiece, *The Decline and Fall of the Roman Empire.* If you ever get a chance to see a picture of Gibbon, notice how his ears were also tilted against his face at an odd angle.

Drastically **TILTED EAR ANGLES** are rare. Another example of this trait plus **low ears** is Nazi propagandist Joseph Goebbels.

Of all the social observers with low ears, my favorite is Thorstein Veblen. Veblen isn't well known to most people outside the sociology field, which is a shame. He had a marvelous appreciation of how ridiculous people could be (though I won't claim he discovered this) and coined the term *conspicuous consumption* to describe showing off with money.

YOUR MIDDLE-OF-THE-ROAD A.M. STATION

Tastes in radio-listening habits haven't been correlated with ear position, so far as I know. But anyone with **AVERAGE-PLACED** ears has the advantage that some of the "easy listenning" stations try to convince you is their exclusive trademark.

Those with **average-placed ears** have easy listening built in! Their pace of thinking meshes with that of the masses. They aren't constantly tempted to interrupt, like **high-eared** listeners. Nor do they suffer from the nagging feeling they're missing something, which can haunt people with **low ears.**

Average-placed ears thus give their owners the gift of good timing. (Interestingly, they are very common in professional baseball players.)

I've also noticed that folks with these ears can have a

knack for tuning in to the average person in the street. Remember the TV jingle "Listen to the heartbeat of America"? That was probably figured out by someone with **average-placed ears.**

Ears of this type belonged to psychoanalyst Sigmund Freud and Erasmus, the great humanist.

To communicate best with any new acquaintance, it's vital to check out ear position and pace yourself accordingly. Begin, of course, by getting a fix on your own ear placement. Remember, look straight into that mirror. Otherwise, you will tilt the ear angle.

Are your ears placed high? Then show mercy and slow down the lightning speed with which you leap from one context of thought to the next (possibly leaving in your wake the rubble from a marathon of mixed metaphors).

Are your ears placed low? Try giving some friendly reassurance that you are, indeed, awake and listening. Even though you may not have instant one-liners to toss out at your audience, a few head nods and "hmm"s may do the trick nicely.

CONFORMITY STYLE

How far the ears stick out reveals another secret.

With experience, you'll develop a knack for judging this. If you're in doubt, look at the ears from the back of the head. Move fancy hairstyles out of the way as needed. Now visualize sliding a pencil between the ear and the head.

It doesn't fit? Then ear angle is "in." It does? The ear angle is "out." What? You could fit in several of your favorite Crayolas side by side? Then ear angle is definitely "far out."

Now, what does it all mean?"

Symbolically, ear angle represents a typical angle for listening to life.

Imagine that the airwaves are filled with messages from society. "Dress like this." "Do that." "Don't speak until you're spoken to." The programming goes on and on.

Now, when folks have ears close to the head, it's as though the messages go straight through the ears, splat into the head. Picture that head nodding "Yes, I get it. I'll obey."

The closer in the ears, the more conformity to the values of society.

Scenario two shows a different style of receiving social messages. This time the catcher's mitt, the ear, is separated farther from the head. So after the catch is made, the response is "Yes, I get it. Now let me decide whether or not I am going to buy into this."

The farther ears stick out, the more independence from social convention.

Don't expect someone whose ears stick out to like going along with the crowd. Even if these natural **NONCONFORMISTS** appear to fit in, they have a need to do things their way, just because they want to. If others don't like it, too bad.

The more ears stick out, the stronger this tendency. Author James M. Barrie had the perfect ears to create Peter Pan, a boy who refused to grow up and conform to expectations for an adult.

Other people with **far-out** ears are the Indian revolutionary leader Mahatma Gandhi and American rocketry pioneer Robert Goddard. Would Oliver North have given the same shredding instructions if his ears stuck out less outrageously? If there was ever a man with Contra ears, it is North!

At the other extreme, ears flat against the head show a person most comfortable when going along with the crowd. Folks with **CONFORMIST EARS** can be very skilled at tact; be aware, in fact, that their sensitivity to social conventions amounts to a talent.

Novelist Charles Dickens, for instance, was able to depict outlandish eccentricity, drawing on nuances of absurdity from real life that a less ardent conformist might never have

Angle

Conformist

Nonconformist

noticed. Sure enough, in the end Dickens's heroes conformed to the values of Victorian society.

Who else has benefited, earwise, careerwise? Contemporary entrepreneur Armand Hammer and philosopher, statesman, and writer José Ortega y Gasset have made brilliant use, in different ways, of their perceptions of society. "Boss"

Tweed, of Tammany Hall, also made skillful (if corrupt) use of the political system of his time.

One of my favorite social observers is **conformist-eared** W. S. Gilbert, whose vast appreciation of absurdity resulted in the wittiest comic operas in the English language.

Of course, the staunchest conservatives don't find nonconformity especially hilarious. I suspect that traditional Siang Mien came from people without a whole lot of humor or nonconformity. All it says about ears that stick out is to dictate this: The closer ears stay to the head, the better.

In fact, Siang Mien doesn't even raise the issue of conformity. Instead, it judges people with stuck-out ears as having emotional troubles. Needless to say, a native nonconformist would have been greatly troubled in the Siang Mien culture.

We Americans owe a lot of our pop culture to nonconformists. Especially our food. There's McDonald's, courtesy of Ray Kroc's maverick ears.

Even before he developed the potential of those golden arches, Kroc had some pretty wacky notions. While a salesman for paper products he came up with the idea of carryout. The restaurant owners scoffed, of course. Who would want to pay good money for restaurant food and not stick around to eat it?

And where would we be without Perdue chickens (thanks to the enterprising ears of Frank Perdue) or Carvel ice cream (courtesy of spunky-eared Thomas Carvel)?

Fannie Farmer, whom today's chefs may not consider terribly trendy, still needed plenty of nerve to found her cooking school back when Boston was a casserole of conservatism. Could she have done it without those independent ears?

Even this brief introduction to nonconformist and conformist ears should suffice to make a point. We need both kinds to make our world.

Sometimes you'll actually see both together in one face, in the case of **COMBINATION EARS.** These are the ears whose tops stick out and bottoms lie flat against the head. Or vice versa. This can be an excellent trait for diplomacy, because such people deeply understand both conformist and nonconformist impulses.

LISTEN BEFORE YOU LEAP

It's always wise to start with self-recognition. Which way do your sympathies, and your ears, lie? Use this knowledge when assessing a stranger's degree of conformity.

By all means, select a new date whose ear angles are similar to your own; and don't wear your T-shirt into the board meeting until you've checked out the local ears (and customs) well in advance. Listen before you leap—or at least watch the angle of their ears.

CHAPTER
5

EYES

Who needs a special textbook to interpret people's eyes? Eyes themselves are a textbook for anyone willing to look. My Face Reading Secrets will show you a facet of personality quite distinct from the mood your subject projects.

Beneath that kindly exterior is your subject as finicky as Morris the cat? As open as a book? Reserved? Suspicious? Prone to intense intimacy? Read on.

WARINESS INDEX

Focus on the shape of the lower eyelids to read the Wariness Index. This shape shows degree of openmindedness. How open is your subject to learning the truth about people and situations, as opposed to judging with preconceived notions?

Here's a simple way to experience for yourself what wariness does to eye shape. Get a mirror handy. Scrunch up your face and glare into it with your most suspicious expression.

"You beast! How dare you tie me to the railroad tracks and confiscate my diary?"

Say whatever it takes to rouse you into a fury. Notice how your lower lids straighten out.

Now pretend you're acting in a love scene, staring infatuatedly at some incredible sex symbol. Open up your face and watch yourself receive a supremely romantic declaration of love.

"Oh, you really think I'm the most attractive, wonderful person you've ever met? Why? When did you first begin to notice?"

Your lower lids should be curving now. They don't call them goo-goo eyes for nothing.

As you just saw, the muscles you use to narrow or round your eyes relate to emotions. Over time, the patterns you use most frequently shape the usual contour of lower eyelids.

The rounder eyes look more appealing, don't they? However, they may not be the easier ones to have. Emotional openness increases a person's likelihood of getting hurt. The more curve to the eyes, the more openness, the greater emotional risk.

What is it like living inside a set of very wary eyes? The cause of wariness may range from shyness to suspicion, anxiety, rage or other emotions that result in being closed off to others. Read **STRAIGHT lower eyelid** as wariness.

This person has the habit of unconsciously filtering out many perceptions about people. Judgmental thinking is the conscious counterpart.

"Did you see that outfit? Forget him." or "What a phony." Strangers get written off and disposed of with a speed proportional to the straightness of those lower eyelids.

This is the potential challenge of this trait. However, the corresponding strength is nothing to sneeze at: loyalty. It's tough to pass the wary one's test, but if you do, you're set for life.

Not that rounder-eyed people never criticize or judge others—but generally they do it after forming a more complete perception. A person with straight lower lids screens out information before it can be consciously evaluated.

Misanthropic humorist Samuel Clemens (known as Mark Twain) had a straight lower lid on his right eye. (His curved left eye let in more information.)

You'll see relatively few famous people with straight lower lids except for politicians, in whom it is fairly common.

Wariness index

Straight   Curved   Round

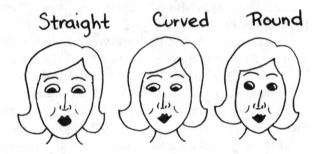

Many people come from families where suspiciousness (and taut lower lids) seems to be passed down as automatically as eye color. For others, wariness has been a perfectly healthy response to painful experiences in life.

I don't mean to imply that wary eyes or the people who

have them are bad. I merely wish to suggest that wary eyes need not stay that way. It took about twenty years (and a lot of emotional work) for my wariness index to switch from straight to curved.

CREATIVITY AND BLUNTNESS

Because **CURVED** lower lids show openness, they are one of the facial signs of creativity. (Different aspects of creativity show in large foreheads, visionary eyebrows, thick eyebrows, far-set eyes, round or flared nostrils, broad chins, and angled brows and chins.)

President Franklin D. Roosevelt, the creative New Dealer who was fabled to have known five thousand people on a first-name basis, kept his wariness down to a graceful curve.

If you look farther back in history, you'll find an open shape to the lower lids of scientist Isaac Newton, poet Dante Alighieri, and Noah Webster, America's first dictionary maker. Two contemporary creative examples are choreographer Jerome Robbins and singer Beverly Sills.

VERY curved lower lids go with **ROUND**, wide-open eyes. They belong to people who let in the most information before censoring it. It's no coincidence that you'll see such eyes on children more often than adults.

Beautiful though these large round eyes may be, don't envy them too fast. Consider the potential challenges: lessons about trust and vulnerability.

Another danger is embarrassing people by being unabashedly watchful, observant, and blunt. (It might be interesting to ask outspoken New York governor Mario Cuomo if he has noticed this.)

Friendships go easier for the wide-eyed one if the mouth is small in size—or else habits of reserve are consciously cultivated.

PUFFS THAT ARE NOT MAGIC

Remember Puff the Magic Dragon? Despite the upbeat theme of this song, dragons aren't famous for happy magic. That certainly holds true for the puff dragons that emerge on faces.

These extra folds of skin start beneath the eyebrow and may hang down as far as the eyelid. In extreme cases, they

Puffs

Low level

Industrial strength

extend even farther, covering part of the eye, forming little tents of flesh.

Puffs reveal discomfort with the environment—ranging from mild physical malaise to Scroogelike hatred of humanity. Not getting enough sleep, overeating (especially foods to which one is allergic), and other strains on the body can produce low-level puffs.

If these trends go uncorrected, the smaller puffs expand into the industrial-strength variety that cover part of the eyes and, symbolically, create a corresponding blindness to part of life.

The typical cause of either size of puff is self-neglect due to focusing hard on other people (pleasing them, helping them, earning money from them, and so forth). The person does not pay attention to messages from the physical body, such as "I'm tired," "I'm full."

Ironically, over time this can result in a feeling of extreme irritability that is detrimental to pleasing those other people.

Puffs are a good example of how you can use Face Reading Secrets. During a job interview, that potential employer may go to great lengths to show he's a nice guy. Once you are on the payroll, his temper will emerge more often than you have been led to expect—unless you were forewarned and fore-armed by reading those puffs.

For the **LOW-LEVEL** puffs, read low-level irritability and fussiness. Small faults in the environment get blown out of proportion.

For certain types of work, of course, a moderate bit of puff can be helpful. We need critics to balance out the airy-fairies. Thank goodness for people like Nancy Austin and Tom Peters, coauthors of *A Passion for Excellence.*

Then come the **INDUSTRIAL-STRENGTH** puffs, so big they look like folds of skin hanging down over the eyeball. Taken in context with the rest of the face, you may read chronic cantankerousness, defensiveness, even selfishness and dishonesty.

Some of our least popular presidents were notable for their imperial puffs: Andrew Johnson, Ulysses Grant, Grover Cleveland, William Howard Taft, Benjamin Harrison, Martin Van Buren, and Millard Fillmore.

Admittedly, some people wear their puffs gracefully. The puff point of view may even be essential to their charm. Would Sir Arthur Conan Doyle have created the same Sherlock Holmes if he hadn't been so persnickety about details? And imagine that rascal W. C. Fields *not* complaining!

Should someone tell you such marks of stress are irreversible or the automatic effect of aging, don't believe it. A holistic approach toward your health can work wonders. That includes healing habits of negative attitudes and speech. In my experience, forgiveness and generosity can get folks farther, over time, than cosmetic surgery.

Take a blink to refresh yourself. Now it's full gaze ahead. There's still plenty more to see.

SETUP

While our attention is still riveted to the upper portion of eyes, let's not neglect some of the basic setup features.

How deep set are your subject's eyes?

Perhaps a more basic question is, how can you tell?

Eye set isn't marked as plainly as the setup key on a computer terminal. It's a relatively subtle consideration.

Look at your subject's eyebone and notice how deeply the eye beneath it fits into the socket. After a few faces you'll get the knack. At one extreme you'll find **DEEP SET EYES**, and at the other, **PROTRUDING EYES.** (Most eyes have **AVERAGE** set.)

The owner of **deep-set** eyes enters into conversation casually, as though she's sitting in a laid-back posture. By contrast, a person with **protruding** eyes gets so caught up in the conversation, it's as if she sits on the edge of her seat.

Set

Protruding

Deep set

Flown out of
socket completely

When the latter type speaks, *do not interrupt.* Because they get so involved when they talk, folks with bulging eyes tend to interpret interruption as an Archie Bunker–like command to "stifle yourself."

Yes, actress Jean Stapleton was perfectly cast as Edith. Such interruptions caused her the greatest humiliation.

As for people with **deep-set** eyes, interruption is no problem. Instead it's getting them to start talking in the first place! Reserved and reticent, they appear to be avid listeners. Don't be fooled, though. They don't necessarily agree with what they hear.

Their listening stance ranges from cautious skepticism to downright suspicion. So if you want to be sure your opinion will be accepted, back it up with proof. Nothing will be taken for granted by those with **deep-set** eyes.

Certainly you wouldn't have wanted to get on the wrong side of that perceptive anthropologist with the deep-set eyes, Dr. Margaret Mead.

Another example is J. D. Salinger, who gave rebellious adolescents of all ages a satisfying role model in Holden Caulfield, hero of *The Catcher in the Rye.*

It's hard to know about Salinger's personality from media interviews. There are none. He's as fastidious about being reclusive as he is about writing. Still, if you're familiar with his writing, don't you have the impression of a taciturn, merciless listener? Very **deep set**!

The strength of **deep-set** eyes is professionalism. Being able to hide your personal opinion can be helpful in the business world, if you are called upon to play the role of uninvolved listener.

TUNNEL VISION

Create for yourself a mental picture of the kind of person who would have tunnel vision. Would you space that person's eyes close together or far apart?

Close together, of course. Folks with eyes set near to the nose are detail-oriented, it's true. They may also have a tendency toward being narrow-minded, not seeing the forest for the trees.

The good news? Their ability to notice individual trees is exceptional.

If you want to locate close- versus far-set eyes in a forest full of subjects, how do you do it? Keep in mind most people have **AVERAGE SET.** You're interested only in the cases where eye set is markedly close or far. Only **VERY**s count.

Basically, if a subject's eyes are clearly as close to the nose as could be, it's **CLOSE SET.** If you find yourself squinting to figure out if eyes are close set or if the subject just has a narrow face—forget it! Go on to a different trait.

Similarly, if eyes are genuinely **FAR SET**, you won't have to force the perception.

When you do find those rare close-set eyes, it pegs an ability worth noticing. These focusers can be terrific golfers, such as Jack Nicklaus and Tommy Armour; astute journalists like Horace Greeley; or masters of musical nuance like soprano Kiri Te Kanawa.

Inventor Thomas Edison had **close-set** eyes. Finally, let's not leave out silversmith Paul Revere and wordsmith William Safire.

As for the folks with **far-set** eyes, don't expect them to excel at observing details. They may even have a tendency to space out (especially if they have **starter** eyebrows). But go to them when you want a broad perspective.

Here are the rangers who see the whole forest. (For them, the challenge can be focusing in and taking action to further their personal needs.)

Eye distance

Far set   Close set

Farsighted William Fulbright, chairman of the U.S. Senate Foreign Relations Committee, took the lead in criticism of foreign military intervention. Margaret Sanger was ahead of her time when she saw the need to make birth control widely available.

Some people with far-set eyes set trends by their personal example. Paul Laurence Dunbar became the first black author to gain national recognition. Composer Ellen Zwilich set a precedent by being the first woman to win the Pulitzer prize for music.

Another woman, Corazon Aquino, sized up the political terrain in her country with surprising results. She led the "people power" revolution that deposed Philippine dictator Ferdinand Marcos. Who would have expected a convent-reared housewife to grow up to be president?

Farsighted imagination has also guided science fiction writer Arthur C. Clarke, most famous for *2001: A Space Odyssey*. Kurt Gödel is a cult hero for some mathematicians. Fashion editor Grace Mirabella has used her foresight to spot trends in fashion.

Let's not leave out the far-set eyes belonging to the superstar who had the vision to realize that he'd be better off wearing only one glove, Michael Jackson.

If I had to pick one pair of **far-set** eyes to represent what makes the people who own them so special, I'd choose Doug Henning. This delightful magician uses his art to give people the experience of wonder.

The more open we are to the broad picture in life, the more we do feel wonder. Of course, it's also necessary to appreciate the small picture—life's practical details. Those of us with average-set eyes do both to some extent. But we can learn a great deal from those with the special gifts of close- and far-set eyes.

EYELID THICKNESS

Without eyelids, our eyes would feel pretty naked. But we don't all have the same amount of eyelid showing from the front. Have you ever taken a good look at the skin directly over the upper eyelashes?

Eyelid thickness reveals something important about your subject's relationship to others.

Let's take a moment to help you find this seldom noticed facial trait. Anatomists call it "tarsal plate," but that probably doesn't help much.

My highly technical term *eyelids* refers to the fold of skin directly above your eyelashes. Say you slather your eyelids with bright green eye shadow. When you open your eyes, the amount of green that shows reflects the size of your eyelid area.

If you put on that eye shadow, would it show enough for you to get your money's worth? Or would the green show only when you blinked?

Take a moment to appreciate the contours of this fascinating part of your face. Is the eyelid barely there, not there at all, or sensuously thick? Do both eyes show the same amount?

Notice that eyelid thickness is *not* the same thing as whether eyelid skin folds over beneath the brow bone. This trait means having either "double eyelids" or "single eyelids." The latter is a common Asian trait (often mistaken for "slanted" eyes—you'll read about eye angle in chapter eleven).

Eyelid thickness is an important trait to notice because it symbolizes a person's comfort zone with intimacy.

Some of us feel more comfortable when we can share the details of our life with someone. We have a large guest room built into the apartment of our personality. Those of us who feel this way probably have **AMPLE EYELIDS.**

With **THIN EYELIDS,** or none at all, a person may learn to share intimate matters, but getting close takes more effort.

To put it bluntly, **NO EYELIDS** is the mark of someone who sees life in terms of self. A loner. A self-made success. At the other extreme, a person with ample lids sees life in terms of self plus significant other. The more generous, the greater the built-in capacity for intimacy.

Some people have left their mark in history because of their compassionate perspective. It shows in their generously proportioned eyelids: President Abraham Lincoln; Alfred Nobel, who endowed the Nobel prizes; President James Madison, masterbuilder of the American Constitution.

A present-day politician, Hawaiian congresswoman Patsy Mink, has **abundant eyelids.** This helps explain the kind of personal magnetism that has made it possible for her to finance running for office entirely through contributions and volunteer help. Her best volunteer? Her husband.

Thick eyelids can also go with sensuality, as in the romantic operas produced by composer Giacomo Puccini.

Eyelids

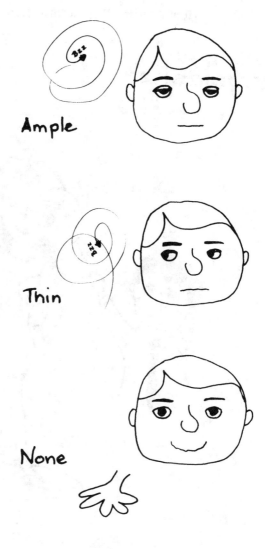

Ample

Thin

None

By contrast, another operatic composer, Richard Wagner, had very **thin eyelids.** His temperament produced more spectacular music, but he didn't exactly specialize in cozy love duets.

Mystery writer Agatha Christie also had thin eyelids. No

Eyelashes

Very fine

doubt it helped her avoid excessive attachment to her ficti-
tious murder victims.

In all fairness, there is a silver lining nestled in the small
space of skimpy eyelids: a clearer capacity to know what you
want for yourself. Whether this winds up as purposeful or
ruthless, eyelids alone don't reveal. It could be a challenge. It
could be a strength.

A potential challenge for one with **ample eyelids** is excessive dependency on that significant other.

FORTY LASHES

One final upper eye feature—have you ever wondered about
eyelashes? I mean, why men often have such thick beautiful
ones while women (the ones under constant siege from the
mascara industry) often don't.

Sorry, I have no answer to that one.

But here's an insight which may provide some consolation.
VERY FINE LASHES demote extreme sensitivity. (Watch out
for hair-trigger temper!) **THICK LASHES** proclaim a more
easygoing temperament.

C H A P T E R
6

NOSES

Are we prying when we read a face? Not really. Admittedly, many folks would freak out if they guessed their face secrets were being studied. What would they cover up first, if they knew what it revealed? Noses.

Nose reading could be considered the nosiest. For one thing, it shows money habits. That's right. Saving and spending styles are right there—and that's just the tip of the noseberg.

Noses also show how your subject handles routine work, accepts financial support from family, and relates to team-work. The face is a living résumé, no doubt about it.

THE TIP TO SAVINGS

The nose tip is the single biggest tip-off to a person's money life. The size gauges the importance of financial security for your subject.

When you browse through a magazine's business pages or watch shows like *MacNeil/Lehrer NewsHour*, you will see many marvelously **BIG**-bulbed noses. Bearing in mind that **VERY** = **VERY**, it should be apparent that the bigger the

Tip

Big

Small

nose tip, the more often your subject thinks (or worries or gloats) about personal savings.

How much money is actually in the bank? Sorry, the nose doesn't tell. The desire for material security doesn't necessarily match the size of your subject's nest egg.

Karl Malden was perfectly cast for the TV commercials about American Express traveler's checks. He owns a schnozz that says "Don't leave home without *money*, plenty of it."

At the other extreme of believable nose casting is Meryl Streep in *Out of Africa*. She plays a heroine, modeled after Danish novelist Isak Dinesen, whose material possessions weigh her down. Exquisite though her belongings are, she has paid for them dearly.

Meryl plays her role brilliantly—all except for her nose, whose tiny tip tells any competent face reader a rather startling secret.

Though Meryl might not choose to admit this in public, I'm willing to bet that holding on to money is one of the last things in the world she considers important. That's what a **SMALL** tip usually signifies.

How about the real Dinesen? Now that's a nose tip! And one with shallow nostrils (you'll read about nostrils later, but can you guess in advance what they signify?).

Who thinks about money most often? People who are very poor, also people who are ambitious, greedy, philanthropic, art collectors. . . . Becoming privy to Face Reading Secrets, you'll find that money-conscious people come from every income bracket. When you meet a **BIG** nose tip, you'll need to look at the rest of the nose to sense the nature of your subject's relationship to money and work.

Keep in mind that people who have inherited wealth may not think about it much. Correspondingly, their nose tips may be small.

Consider the modest tip of Dina Merrill. Her acting career is notable for how long it has lasted . . . and for how little she's needed the money.

Her father founded E. F. Hutton. Her mother, Marjorie Merriweather Post, brought another fortune into the family coffers. No doubt Ms. Merrill is one of the wealthiest women ever to choose an acting career.

NOSTRILS LIKE A PIGGY BANK

Remember piggy banks? They have narrow slots to hold the coins you deposit. Most of us throw our loose change into a container with easier access, like a jar or a desk drawer.

Nostrils can be likened to the slot in a bank. Some people choose a big slot, for easy cash flow. Others prefer a narrow slot, to make every penny count.

To put it bluntly, bigger spenders have BIGger nostrils. Those who spend less have SMALLer nostrils.

How can you measure nostril proportions without making yourself conspicuous?

It's easy. When the whole nostril shape shows from a front view, on a level angle, count the nostrils as large. The air holes you can barely see from the front are the ones considered small.

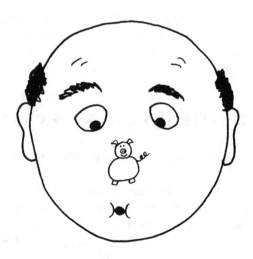

Some of the world's richest people have matched huge nose tips with teensy nostrils.

Alexander Hamilton, America's first Secretary of the Treasury, had such a nose. The tradition carried on with entrepreneur Andrew Carnegie, banker J. P. Morgan, railway magnate James J. Hill, Today we have Aldo Gucci, manufacturer of the famous status accessories.

John D. Rockefeller would seem to be an exception to this rule. The nose tip may be substantial, but its proportions are rivaled by some of the largest nostrils I've ever seen. Well, wouldn't you know it, this steel tycoon wasn't just famous for bringing in the loot. He was a passionate philanthropist.

The folks with **small** nostrils to go with **big** tips don't merely hold on to wealth themselves, they can help others do it. Ralph Nader has fought for consumerism. So has makeup expert Paula Begoun, known as "The Ralph Nader of rouge."

Arthur Frommer has guided travelers to see the world for less. Lee Iacocca has raised money for the Statue of Liberty. Jane Bryant Quinn has shared financial advice in her writings.

Mahatma Gandhi and Mother Teresa exemplify that personal vows of poverty do not imply lack of interest in helping others overcome financial problems.

DELVING INTO NOSTRILS

Now, if you aren't squeamish, let's continue to delve into nostrils.

Nostril shape should be read in conjunction with size. Just as nostrils size shows *amount* of spending, their shape shows characteristic *quality* of spending style.

If the Lord loves a cheerful giver, folks with **ROUND** nos-

trils must have front-row pews reserved in heaven. Their money style is resourceful. They find creative ways to finance the flow of spending.

When a woman with **VERY huge, round** nostrils attended one of my workshops, I suggested gently that she might be a lavish spender with a knack for juggling her debts. She exploded with laughter. Eventually she calmed down, gasping: "I have twenty-two credit cards, and they're all charged up to the limit. So my nostrils gave me away, did they?"

FLARED nostrils are the ones that widen from the nose center outward. The owners of the flared nostrils spend with flair. They are adventurous . . . risk takers, even. Spending money seems to bring more pleasure to them than to other people.

How do you read the combination of **small, flared** nostrils? These folks are relatively good at sticking to a budget. When they choose to spend, though, they live it up.

Shallow nostrils with a **RECTANGULAR** or square shape go with conventional patterns of spending. Usually, these nostrils are also small. Expect their owners to excel at economizing. If rich, they may enjoy hiding how much they have.

Look out for the rare nostrils that appear **TRIANGULAR.** These pinched outlets for air parallel pinched spending patterns.

Stinginess. That may be how the spending patterns look to an outsider. A more compassionate view for an insider to take is that there has been a history of perpetual scarcity. It marks the habit of not being a have-it.

The inquiries I have made among people with this facial characteristic have confirmed that serious financial difficulties, plus being cut off from family support, figured traumatically in that person's past.

The expectation of lack can become a self-fulfilling prophecy.

I believe that money attitudes directly affect personal wealth. Not everyone buys this concept—especially folks with triangular nostrils.

For those who are open to the idea of changing attitudes to create long-term prosperity, there are some marvelous books and seminars in the marketplace. I'd recommend three books for starters: *Think and Grow Rich* by Napoleon Hill; *The Dynamic Laws of Prosperity,* by Catherine Ponder; and *Moneylove* by Jerry Gillies. Possibly, over time, the effort to build a prosperity consciousness will broaden the nostrils along with their owner's outlook.

Meanwhile, **triangular** nostrils can be helpful for certain professions. Witness the success of economist Paul Anthony Samuelson and banker John Heimann. Feisty congressman Claude Pepper used his sense of financial scarcity to defend the savings of senior citizens.

Perhaps this chapter will inspire you to make nostrils one of the first things you notice in a face. When you spot those **flared**, adventurous nostrils, don't be surprised at the rampant creativity that can breathe through them.

There's Clare Boothe Luce, whose multifaceted career has included being a congresswoman, diplomat, and columnist. There's award-winning architect I. M. Pei. And many more.

Nostril traits, like all other facial traits, can be read as positive or negative: Either strengths or challenges can prevail. Take the shallow nostrils that, as we've heard, denote relatively joyless spending. Fasten them onto the soul of a man like Senator William Proxmire and wow! Someone created one of the most vigorous and responsible nonspenders we've ever had in American government.

What if the most pinched nostril shape combines with a huge nostril size? How can you sort out the mixed message of "don't spend" with "spend it all"? In the few cases I've seen, that mixed message was, in itself, the subject's challenge.

FAMILY TREE

The nose broadens out at either side of the nostrils to symbolize financial roots—the contribution of family and friends to your subject's support.

The "roots" of this family tree are the flaps of skin that cover up nostrils. Admittedly, you're probably not used to thinking of them that way, if you think of them at all. Another perspective is to think of them as the sides of the nose tip.

Nose roots

Ample

Skinny

Grooved

Smooth

However you think of them, take a good look at your nose roots now. They are an often overlooked but rather interesting feature.

Check both the size of the roots and how smoothly they join onto the major trunk of the nose.

Root size reveals amount of support; joining symbolizes how smoothly your subject connects up with the support.

Fleshy, full roots, symbolizing great potential support from loved ones, won't do your subject much good unless they join smoothly. When a line separates roots and tip, interpret that as a wall between your subject and the family coffers. I refer to this as a **GROOVE.**

A groove can be a very faint line or a deep demarcation. The length of the groove may vary too. It may go partway down the side of the root or, in rare cases, extend all the way down. A thick line that extends the full length of each root counts as a **VERY big groove**!

Happily, most noses show a smooth joining, symbolizing strong family support.

Comedian Bill Cosby is my idea of a hunk, and part of the credit goes to his wonderful hunk of a nose, with its **AMPLE ROOTS**, seamlessly attached. Here, you feel, is a man who gets and gives plenty of family support. The structure of his eyes enhances the warmth built into his face. Ample eyelids suggest a wonderful instinct for sharing with others.

By contrast, photographer Diane Arbus's nose had **SKIMPY** roots, cut off from the tip of the nose by deep grooves. Appropriately, her specialty as a photographer was people who fit in freakily with their surroundings. They appear cut off from society's support.

One of the most inspiring sets of nose roots, if I may say such a thing, belongs to Pope John Paul II. Next time you see a picture of him—or he comes to visit—check out those magnificent nose flanges and how smoothly they blend into the tip. He's a superb gatherer of support for and from his church family.

If you want to peek at a subject's style of intimacy, three parts of the face should be considered in combination. Look at the thickness of eyelids for how much your subject is prepared to give. Nose roots show how much your subject receives. And the extent to which ears stick out shows how much your subject is prepared to compromise for the sake of closeness.

NOSE TO THE GRINDSTONE

Quick quiz: Which kind of nose is traditional for aristocrats, long or short?

LONG, of course—but did you ever wonder why?

Do noses get transmitted like a family name, along with write-ups in the *Social Register* and silver spoons? Can you tell an "old money" nose at a glance? Not necessarily. Life isn't that simple.

But guess what, work styles are! They can be as plain as the length of nose on your face.

I look at it this way. Breathing is a basic human job. Everyone has to get the same amount of breath through the nose—enough to live. Some noses are designed to get this work done directly, with no frills. These are the **SHORT**, get-down-to-business noses.

Other breathing machines are designed to get the work done more decoratively. Style matters as much as function. These are the more ornamental long noses. Work habits correspond accordingly—less rush, more style.

As the accompanying illustration shows, neither nose has an edge in terms of intimidation. Short and long noses, both, can go with people who are angry, busy, hardworking— you name it.

Personally, I'd love to see an end to the ways that people from different social classes look down their noses at each other. Maybe it will help to spell out the special qualities that go with both work styles, short-nosed and long-nosed.

SHORT noses come with a special gift: a talent for old-fashioned hard work. They excel at productivity on a routine basis.

Go ahead. Search any organization. Regardless of job title, the ones who work hardest, day in and day out, have the shortest noses.

The potential challenge with such noses is being taken for granted. "Of course Sheila will do it. That's her job." "No

Nose length

need to thank him for all that overtime—Jeff's so dependable, he always works hard."

Should you be one of those habitually hardworking **short**-nosed folks, here's my recommendation: Counteract that potential challenge by demanding recognition occasionally.

(P.S.: If people give you compliments, accept them. Otherwise, how are you going to get them trained?)

The ones who keep their nose to the everyday grindstone may be clericals or executives. In the nonpaid world of labor, they may be conscientious mothers on welfare or DAR members who volunteer for the Junior League.

Whatever their income bracket, people with short noses are tops at dealing with the unglamorous necessities of the work world.

Many advocates for working-class people are notable for their short noses: Jacob Riis, author of *How the Other Half Lives;* William Jennings Bryan, known as "The Commoner"; attorney Clarence Darrow, who first won fame as a labor lawyer; and labor organizers Samuel Gompers and Mother Jones.

Artist Norman Rockwell, the prolific artist, was also a member of the short-nose society.

One of my favorites is Chief Justice Earl Warren, whose nose was as cute as a button. He oversaw the Supreme Court's landmark decision in favor of school desegregation. Warren once said he wanted to be remembered as Justice of "the people's court."

LONG IN THE NOSE

What is the special excellence of the **long**-nosed worker?

Quite frankly, routine work it probably isn't. The longer your nose, the more you probably suffer in the kind of job at which short-nosed workers excel.

Your forte is strategy rather than routine work. A different kind of creativity is involved here. Unlike the creative expediting of work, at which short noses excel, the longer-nosed specialty is long-term original projects.

And planning the task is half the fun.

Witness naturalist pioneer John James Audubon; Renaissance man Sir Francis Bacon; Chief Joseph, one of the greatest Native American strategists; and Walter Bagehot, the founder of British political sociology.

HOW YOU MAKE IT LONG

I'm reminded of the cigarette ad that proclaims, "It's not how long you make it, it's how you make it long." They could have been talking about noses! Because nose shape is fully as significant as size. It shows personal style in the workplace— the way a person will work most effectively.

When you see a **STRAIGHT** nose, it's like peeking at someone's business ID card. It says, "Logic at work."

These folks are in their element when they can analyze the steps of a project and work through them systematically. They love to follow procedures.

What they don't like is being asked to work without (logical) rhyme or reason, such as cosmetic handling of job problems. Their potential challenge with others is intolerance for those who work in a nonlogical style.

When a nose is both **STRAIGHT AND LONG**, expect intellectual brilliance, with long-term development of ideas.

Author Ernest Hemingway's prose style reflects his ruthlessly **straight** nose.

Other people whose careers have benefited from the winning combination of **long and straight** are aviator Charles Lindbergh; Sequoyah, who single-handedly developed the Cherokee alphabet; Supreme Court Justice Charles Evans Hughes; Booker T. Washington, founder of Tuskegee Institute; physicist Isaac Newton; and mathematician Benjamin Banneker.

Also, guess what shape of a nose designed the relentlessly perpendicular, soaring skyscrapers known as the New York World Trade Center? You get one point if you guess **straight**. Add a couple of extra points if you also can name the architect—Minoru Yamasaki.

Nose shape

Arched   Bumpy   Ski jump   Straight

VALENTINES AT WORK

Definition first: a **SKI JUMP** nose has an overall shape that scoops inward. (Don't confuse this with separate traits like upturned nose tip, to be discussed later.) This inward angle tells you: "Valentine at work. Feelings count here."

These noses signal a need to check in with feelings and intuition. Having to follow procedures mechanically makes these people miserable. Instead of coffee breaks, they benefit from tune-in time.

"How is this going for me? Do I feel good about this work? If something feels hollow, or otherwise wrong, what do I need to do differently?"

Not only do folks with this nose shape benefit from feeling emotionally good about what they are doing, more than others they need to receive positive strokes from the outside. When an employer praises them in a way they can interpret emotionally as appreciation, productivity increases.

Admittedly, work style and tempo may seem erratic to a ski jump's supervisor. These people operate on the basis of their feelings, meaning when they're hot, they're hot; when they're not, they're not. This is not a straight-nosed, even flow of energy.

For decades, comedian Bob Hope has used **ski jump** logic to give a lift to his jokes. Artists in other genres also may credit success to the kind of emotion-based logic that shows in a ski jump nose.

Here's how singer John Denver has described what makes his work unique: "I am singing about how good it is to be alive."

Other **ski jump** artists are painter Mary Cassatt, guitarist Andrés Segovia, novelist Willa Cather, and movie star Leslie Caron.

Norman Cousins owes his health, as well as his greatest fame, to the discovery that laughter can challenge the grim logic of disease.

GUMPTION BUMPS
AND VIOLINS

BUMPS in noses symbolize unique, individual kinds of logic for work. This can be misinterpreted as lack of logic, but shouldn't be.

Jean-Jacques Rousseau, the educational philosopher who so influenced the romantic movement in literature, was criticized for inconsistent logic. Actually, he smashed the boundaries of fossilized convention.

A more contemporary example is Duke Ellington, whose individualistic style at jazz also qualifies as boundary smashing.

For better or worse, nose bumps represent individualistic logic at work. If the bump lies at the bridge, where the noses starts, individualism is strongest at the start of a project. A bump halfway down symbolizes the need to use individualistic logic halfway through a project. And so on.

How about the bumps from broken noses—do they count? You bet. If a fighter has taken a lot of lumps, it may be that his thinking is affected, not just his nose. I think of them as bumps of gumption.

Most of the shapes people call bumps on their noses are really small arches. The amount of arch in **ARCHED** noses can vary from slight to enormous. Read it as the ability—and need—for elegant creativity at work.

Creativity takes many forms. I define it as finding unique, one-of-a-kind solutions that make greatest use of the resources available.

Physicists call it elegance. Economists call it economy. For artists, this nose shape is associated with a deep love of beauty. I think of cellist Pablo Casals, composer Aaron Copland, choreographer Agnes de Mille, and singer/songwriter Aretha Franklin.

Fans of singer Barbra Streisand will be quick to point out all the art in her nose.

Then there's Gordon Parks, a versatile creator of beauty who has excelled not only as a musician but also as a poet and photographer.

EVERYDAY PADDING

Finally, as you assess what noses say about work style, don't forget the padding. From a front view, can you see a prominent bone down the center?

If not, you're looking at a thicker nose. You may see it as a **PADDED** nose, from bridge to tip. This padding indicates good teamwork ability on the job. These are the folks who get energy and enthusiasm from working with others.

By contrast, an **UNPADDED** nose with the bone showing reveals a streak of independence. These folks hate to have someone looking over their shoulder. The thinner the nose, the more personal space they need.

Being a self-starter is the strength. The potential challenge is being viewed as aloof—or feeling lonely.

Greta Garbo, the reclusive actress, no doubt benefited from her nose when delivering her famous line "I want to be alone."

President Woodrow Wilson was hardly reclusive, but he was fiercely independent, as was conservationist John Muir.

Later on you'll read about cheek padding, which symbolizes something related—support from others for leadership.

Nose padding

Padded   Unpadded

The distinction is that the nose padding reflects personal comfort zone for working with others. Cheek padding shows effectiveness at gaining support from others.

CURIOSITY—THE TIP-OFF

So, we've now scrutinized nostrils, nose shape, length, and padding. At the start of this chapter we focused on nostrils. I hope you don't feel in danger of getting sick of the subject. To me it's forever fascinating.

(Did you know, by the way, that *nosology* is the name for the classification of diseases? Hmm, I wonder what kind of grumpy nose-hater thought up that one.)

Let's go back and look at the tip once more, this time for its angle rather than its size. The **tip** is the place where the nose comes to a point. Compare that location to the **bottom** of the nose, at the base of the nostrils, directly between them. Relative to the bottom, does the tip go up, straight, or down? That's **nose-tip angle.**

NOSES TURN UP

Remember the **TURNED-UP** nose celebrated in the song "Has Anybody Seen My Gal?" This tip shape goes with impetuous speech, impulsive career moves, and . . . an all-around good time. No, actually I meant to say: potential difficulty with keeping secrets. Also, money may get spent as though it had an impetuous life of its own.

All this adds up to an intense curiosity. **VERY upturned** equals very inquisitive.

If the upturned tip is **POINTED** in shape, the owner has a high level of sensitivity to accompany the inquisitiveness. It's the reporter's proverbial "nose for news." Pulitzer prize–winning biographer Tyler Dennett had it, and so does today's irrepressible TV reporter Sam Donaldson.

Speaking of television, did you catch the PBS miniseries about fictional heroine *Anne of Green Gables*? Actress Megan Fol-

Nose tip angle

Turned up   Straight   Turned down   Turned into a dog

lows played the role to perfection—every scene of impulsive, unintentional mischief. The part was perfect for her **upturned** nose tip.

In real life, consumers owe a lot to Ralph Nader and he, in turn, may owe a great deal to his form of nosiness.

FEMINIST NOSE TIPS

If you think back to the Doris Day movies of the *Lover Come Back* era (late 1950s and early 1960s), you may remember the kind of woman she played: impetuous, spunky, and possessing the enduring toughness of a well-roasted marshmallow.

Day's slim, upturned nose was type cast!

I find it intriguing that virtually all the major feminists have had a nose tip with a sturdy **STRAIGHT**forward angle.

It figures that they opted for making their personal and career choices in a solid, dependable way.

The list of such feminists includes Susan B. Anthony, Elizabeth Cady Stanton, Lucy Stone, Carrie Chapman Catt, Frances Perkins, Emmeline Pankhurst, Mary Church Terrell, and Betty Friedan.

THE LOWDOWN ON LOW NOSES

From time to time you'll find a nose tip that sticks out and **TURNS DOWN** lower than the norm. This denotes a strength of deliberateness in making career choices. These people have a healthy sense of their own self-interest.

For a great political leader like Lech Walesa, the interest of a group of people may be treated like a personal concern.

The emotional detachment and shrewdness that go with this nose tip may be an advantage for your subject, but he would be wise to guard against behavior that others will criticize as calculating or selfish.

Evidently Henry Ford had this sort of challenge. His nose was long and straight, with a tip pointing markedly down.

Ford was able to build up his car business with logic and determination, but he wasn't necessarily popular among his workers. Eventually, he collided with the forces of organized labor. At the time, his reputation for generosity was totaled.

As for a **VERY downturned** tip that is extremely **POINTED** in shape, treachery is possible. Certainly, you can be sure these people will be intense to work with.

Basil Rathbone's nose, for instance, made him a wonderful Sherlock Holmes. His nose contributed to his image of ruthless deductive reasoning.

Remember the nose of the Wicked Witch of the West in *The Wizard of Oz*, or the nose on the spiteful witch in Disney's cartoon version of *Snow White*? Long, drooping noses represent selfishness to our collective consciousness.

For the rare person who has such a nose, the challenge may actually be having to prove one's character in the face of others' distrust.

My favorite example of a **downturned** nose belongs to author Ayn Rand, who has gone so far as to preach the virtue of selfishness. Perfect! Here's someone elaborately defending a trait that's as plain as the nose on her face.

CHEEKS

With noses, we started to view the power structures of the face. To get a complete power profile, you will also need to read cheeks, jaws, and chins.

All human beings are powerful. The question is how that power operates. Cheeks reveal which style of leadership suits your subject best.

DEFINITELY CHEEKBONES

Cheeks that stick out conspicuously are the mark of a bold leader. The whole person—not just cheeks—tends to stick out in a crowd.

So you see, it's no coincidence that so many of the performers we watch on TV and movies display powerful cheeks. These are people who love the limelight.

By contrast, if you walk into a grittier setting, say, the cubbyholes of a corporate office building, you'll see folks with the incognito cheeks most of us wear.

One beautiful example of high, **PROMINENT** cheekbones belongs to Katharine Hepburn. She is famous for her feisty screen roles and equally remarkable for her behind-the-scenes

Cheek prominence

Prominent   Incognito

battle with a palsy condition. For years Hepburn has countered a tendency for her voice to shake—steadying it by force of will for most scenes but letting it go for dramatic effect where appropriate. Is that courage or what?

Meanwhile, have you ever wondered why America has never elected a president who looked like Robert Redford? (Even Vice-President Dan Quayle, alleged by some to look like Redford, bears no resemblance around the cheeks.)

Actually, prominent cheeks are a disadvantage for high-level politics. Traditionally, Americans have not been big on cheeky presidents. So far, we have elected just one. Abe Lincoln. It's significant that prominent cheeks have very little padding.

PADDED POWER

PADDED cheeks (i.e., those surrounded by flesh) may not be glamorous, but they indicate the ability to marshal community support—the more padding, the more support. By contrast, jealousy enters the picture when **prominent** cheeks are accentuated by being **UNPADDED.**

Think, for instance, of Cher; Diana, princess of Wales; Jackie Onassis or Nancy Reagan. The tabloids go to town on these ladies. Whether you personally like them or not, I think all of us can sympathize with the amount of gossip per capita.

When your face structure flaunts your power (exceptionally high social status, wealth, or political influence), the backlash can be unpleasant. But the more **FAR SET** the cheeks, the greater the long-term courage.

Some leaders who had to fight essentially lonely battles for years have had *unpadded, far-set* cheeks: Nelson Mandela, South African opponent of apartheid; Geronimo, the famous Apache warrior; Clara Barton, the loner who founded the Red Cross; and Harriet Tubman, known as "the Moses of her people" for her work with the Underground Railroad. These heroes showed the long-term courage that can accompany **prominent, far-set** cheeks.

A present-day warrior with magnificent cheeks is Dr. Elisabeth Kübler-Ross. Her pioneering work on "death awareness" has led to important discoveries that have helped countless people and their families.

With more cheek padding, a person's leadership abilities are better concealed by behavior. Others don't feel so jealous or threatened and are more likely to cooperate. Perhaps such cheeks helped Costa Rican president Oscar Arias Sánchez to win the Nobel prize. Helen Keller, likewise, had her challenges softened by support from others—as symbolized by cheek padding.

Under-cheek area

Unpadded   Padded

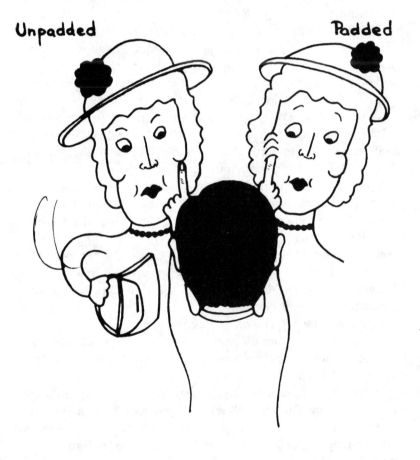

Environmentalist Rachel Carson's broad cheeks were wonderfully padded. Her face typified the padded-power approach: "We've got a great team here. Won't you join us?"

People with padded cheeks tend to be less demanding and critical of other people. *Apple on cheek* doesn't necessarily go with *chip on shoulder*—but it can.

When you read a face with outstanding cheeks, you may find it appropriate to remind your subject that it's a challenge to handle power when it shows conspicuously. Even people ignorant of face reading usually get a clear subconscious message about this form of power.

Of course a champion fighter like Mike Tyson may not mind who notices those powerhouse cheeks.

And what if subject complains, "My cheeks are padded because I'm fat"? Fat does not get distributed equally. Roseanne Barr's chubby cheeks just accentuate their prominence. Whatever is on the face counts, regardless of weight, age, and other excuses people offer to explain away how they look.

SPECIAL OOMPH

How do you read cheekbones that are fuller toward the nose than toward the ears? **CLOSE-SET** cheeks go with a knack for handling short-term projects. These are the people who perform magnificently under pressure.

Give them a project to complete in three hours or three days; leave the three-year or thirty-year assignments to the folks with the Clara Barton cheeks.

You may have noticed these oomphy cheeks on outstanding athletes such as basketball player Bill Walton, Olympic swimmer Mary T. Meagher, and golfer Sam Snead.

No doubt Thomas Gallaudet used the extra oomph in his cheeks to leap over hurdles when he founded America's first free school for the deaf.

Close-set cheeks

Close set   Very close set

PASSION, MEET PACIFISM AND POLITENESS

Sometimes fledgling face readers expect that cheeks are always the broadest part of a face. Look again! Aside from the **LEADERLIKE** faces with cheeks as the widest part, there are three other face shapes.

First are the triangle-shaped faces, where a broad forehead tapers down to a narrow chin. The forehead is considerably broader than the cheeks.

These **PASSIONATE** folks are usually Type A personalities. They move quickly, talk quickly, give vent to anger quickly.

Face proportion

Leaderlike

Passionate

Pacifist

Polite

They want what they want when they want it. They get things done fast.

The strength of this rarest of face shapes is dynamism. The challenge is burning out those who work with them. This is a leadership style you won't forget if you have had to deal with it!

Arsenio Hall accentuates his face shape with his haircut, and brings a correspondingly unforgettable, manic glee to his TV capers.

Alan Alda brought passionate intensity to his role as Hawkeye in *M*A*S*H*.

Werner Erhard used this dynamic style of leadership to found the est training and The Forum.

Two writers with the most contrasting styles you can imagine have benefited from this fiery face shape: Poet Nikki Giovanni and romantic novelist Daphne Du Maurier.

Many people's under-the-cheek area is broader than the cheeks themselves. I call this the **PACIFIST** face shape.

These folks may not necessarily be Type B personalities, but they give the impression that they are the world's "nice guys."

Their talent is to defuse tension. While others are fussing and fuming, the pacifists smooth things over, often by joking. This style of leadership gains respect over time. It's different from the hit-'em-over-the-head Leaderlike and Passion methods—more like hit 'em with a hug.

Leo Buscaglia, "Mr. Hug" himself, is a great example. Buscaglia makes all of that hugging look easy. And genuine.

Other Pacifists may have a harder time sorting out their need to please others from their real feelings. They're so good at holding down negativity that they may stuff their own grumblings—until the buildup gets so bad that they explode.

I suspect that people with this trait benefit more than others from assertiveness training.

Whether or not they overcome the challenge of assertiveness, Pacifists have the gift of outer calmness. Thank God for these people, who can seem placid when others around them are getting hysterical. You'll want to have one around in a crisis.

Bob Hoskins played a perfect Pacifist in *Who Framed Roger Rabbit*. Just think how much provocation he took, from "Toons" and others, before getting visibly upset.

Mind you, there's no psychological law that Pacifist faces can never learn how to voice their gripes. Once they get started, some Pacifists can really get into it. People on the receiving end may feel like they've been hit by a ten-ton truck—while observers *not* on the receiving end may find it remarkably entertaining.

Witness the popularity of Pacifists-turned-critics on TV, such as film reviewer Gene Shalit. Pacifists aren't necessarily pushovers.

Then there are faces where the cheeks lie so flat, they are hard to notice. In a crowd these faces are usually hard to notice too. Their strength is the **POLITE** style of their leadership.

Here are people better adjusted than others to the reality of group dynamics: although each of us is the most important person in our life, we can't all get to play leader. The role of follower is cast far more often.

Naturally more assertive than the Pacifists, the Polite leaders feel free to voice their opinions, positive or negative. They win respect through the gifts of emotional honesty, ability to share, and a relatively easy time with good manners.

These folks don't feel a compulsion to stand in the spotlight, taking credit. They see the job and get it done.

Behavioral psychologist Dr. B. F. Skinner was a good example of this. In a workmanlike way he produced his experiments, promulgated his theories, and responded to critics with grace. He stuck to his world view. He made it work for him.

Which of the four power styles is most important? Admittedly, the Leaderlike style tends to get the most credit in our society, but each style deserves recognition We need them all.

C H A P T E R
8

JAWS

Just when you thought it was safe to go back in the water . . . it's no coincidence that sharks have big jaws. On humans big jaws reveal considerable physical stamina and the need to dominate.

Just how big are **BIG** jaws? Big enough to stash away several wads of chewing gum and still not have it show.

A better guideline is this: If you can look at someone's head from the back and see the corners of the jaws stick out, that's big.

No wonder the Superman image includes huge jaws. Actor Christopher Reeve had the perfect jaws for the job. In Rambo movies, macho Sylvester Stallone had many opportunities to flex his rippling jaws.

Movie stars aren't the only performing artists who depend on physical perseverance. Strong-jawed Seiji Ozawa has been famed for his vigorous style as an orchestral conductor. Director Ron Howard and *Today* show co-host Bryant Gumbel also have built careers with their jowly spunk.

As for Walter Payton, all-time leading rusher for the National Football League, his own brand of artistry bears the stamp of monumental jaws. (Most professional football players are strong on jaws, actually.)

Another dramatic example is best-selling author Louis

L'Amour. Can you imagine the sheer physical stamina needed to knock off eighty-six western novels in one lifetime!

Aside from physical stick-to-itiveness, strong-jawed people are gifted with fierce loyalty and passionate integrity. They can be downright unshakable. World War II heroes Winston Churchill and Dwight D. Eisenhower had such jaws, as did the author of *Profiles in Courage*, President John F. Kennedy.

Of course, men aren't the only ones with big jaws. Some outstanding feminine specimens are Sally Ride, America's first woman astronaut, and Juliette Low, an aristocratic southern belle who shocked people by her determined efforts to found the Girl Scouts.

No reading of jaws would be complete without a quick check for tension. Are they clenched or relaxed? Here's where you see anger stored. For instance, the rage in Marlee Matlin's clenched jaws helped make her convincing as the indomitable heroine of *Children of a Lesser God*.

CHINS

When I ask new students which feature they read most often, the eyes have it. Yet the feature they read most correctly is chins.

Admittedly, chins aren't as glamorous. Nonetheless, they tell an important tale. We sense that a "strong" chin predicts perseverance; a "weak" chin, submissiveness. And, indeed, chins are the face's bottom line—the place where we read instinct.

What will your subject do when push comes to shove? Will it be fight or flight?

For the most thorough interpretation, however, remember to watch chins in conjunction with cheeks and noses. Noses, you'll remember, reveal stamina in work life and (through nostrils) energy spending. Cheeks show how someone will stick out in a crowd. Chins will give you insights into willpower, aggression, and endurance.

How big is your subject's drive? How strong his survival ability? The personal cost of leadership without a lot of chin can be very high. To size up your subject's style in dealing with competitive situations, compare chins.

FIGHTER CHINS

Look at the face in profile, starting with the forehead, and watch the way the whole face slopes downward. It isn't enough to watch from the nose down. In some faces, the whole head angles out dramatically, from forehead to chin. Although the chin size is small, read that chin angle as **VERY PROMINENT.**

Aggression

Average   Receding   A very prominent chin

A **prominent** chin correlates with readiness to compete. This is where you will read willpower. Sticking out = no fear of fighting to win.

Feisty chins show in the faces of social work pioneer Jane Addams, composer Sergei Prokofiev, and General John Pershing.

John Dewey had a **prominent** chin. Another philosopher, Henri Bergson, had a **RECEDING** one. Perhaps the latter model of chin is more what you'd expect of a professional philosopher. But remember, Face Reading Secrets doesn't predict a subject's profession. It gives insight into the *way* the work is done.

If you're involved in yacht racing, you can appreciate how Dennis Conner's style of aggression makes him a winner. Or if racing cars is more your speed, watch how Cale Yarborough brings his strong-chinned style into the Daytona 500.

Jay Leno certainly qualifies for the major leagues of chins. As a comedian, his rapid-fire, nonstop delivery is an excellent example of aggressive humor. This man does not want to stop for breath until he has made you breathless with laughter.

The potential challenge with any of these people is unnecessary aggression. Don't rule out humility—but don't bet on it, either.

What about **receding** chins? What a mistake to call them "weak." After all, was First Lady Eleanor Roosevelt weak?

No, the **receding** angle just shows a challenge with physical aggression. Far from feeling they can bowl the world over (striking terror into the hearts of all ten pins at once), folks with these chins prefer to avoid competition at all costs.

Consequently, they tend to be self-effacing and self-reliant. Assuming they learn the lesson of self-respect, these folks can be a lot more lovable than the huge-chinned Tarzan types.

SURVIVAL OF THE CHINNEST

At this point we could expect the Chris Everts of the sports world to interrupt:

What about those who play a defensive game? Offensive attack isn't the only way to win.

Quite true, and to see who specializes in staying power, look at a chin head-on. How wide is it?

Width of chin symbolizes endurance, the ability to "take it on the chin." **BROAD** chins belong to survivors. These people bounce back from financial challenge, shrug off public criticism, and bear their private burdens stoically.

You don't have to be a tennis player like Chris to find a broad chin indispensable.

No doubt talk show hosts Oprah Winfrey and Phil Donahue depend on the endurance built into their chins. If you look farther back in show business you'll see many examples of people whose success hung on their ability to take it on the chin.

Composer Cole Porter might never have made it without his sizable chin. His first Broadway show was a total flop. And thank goodness Fred Astaire had his chin. Who knows the number of times he fell down! I, for one, am glad he picked himself up and kept on dancing. Ditto for Gene Kelly.

A **LONG** chin, like Astaire's, shows as much staying power as a broad one like Kelly's. Folks with the broad chins get their endurance through feeling connected with others. The long chins tap into endurance through a sense of personal control. So if a chin is long or broad or both, you can read the overall significance as the same.

Consider May Kunin, who came to the U.S. as a refugee from Nazi persecution. The mettle in her long chin has certainly been tested. She survived confrontation after confrontation and managed to become governor of the State of Vermont.

Stamina

Broad   Long   Broad   Delicate
                     and long

Another of my favorite illustrations of chin willpower is the story of actress Patricia Neal. After three years of struggle following a stroke that left her unable to walk or talk, she resumed her career and went on to win an Academy Award nomination.

At this point you may wonder, what happens when chin strength is absent from a face? The person must depend on—or develop—other strengths. Perhaps, too, the challenges faced in life are of a different order. Greenhouse roses don't have to face the elements, the way roses that grow in someone's front yard do.

An interesting face in terms of life work belongs to Dr. Chien-shiung Wu. Her chin is **SMALL.** Yet the upper portion of her face makes up for it. Dr. Wu has been called "the queen of nuclear physics."

Can she tap-dance? I doubt it. However much endurance she has in her personal life, though, her intellect is rigorous. When it comes to staging contests among teeny-tiny particles, this woman is an Amazon.

The strength that goes with a small chin is a hardworking conscience. These people can have intensely strong ethical and moral standards. By the same token, they can be intensely self-critical. Stealing so much as a paperclip from the office can set off tremendous guilt.

Small-chinned folks can also be faced with a related challenge: handling criticism from others. Most already have the equivalent of a Ph.D. in self-criticism.

On the other hand, the challenge of the larger chins can be looser standards of conduct. If these folks get frequent practice taking criticism, could they be doing something to earn it?

SEXY CHINS

Siang Mien observes that **VERY BROAD** chins go with a very developed interest in sex, while smaller chins accompany less sexual drive. If you think in terms of the battle of the sexes, doesn't this makes sense? Those who keep entering the contest again and again are built with the strongest recovery mechanisms.

Two sexual survivors with broad chins are Marabel Morgan, who gained both fans and foes by encouraging wives to become *The Total Woman*; and Sydney Biddle Barrows, the Mayflower Madam.

CHOOSING CAUSES

Apart from aggression and stamina, chins reveal one more thing about your subject's fighting style. What kinds of causes are considered worth fighting for?

To find out, look at the shape of those chins.

As with eyebrows, there are three main shapes. The same three shapes, in fact: **curved, straight** (sometimes called "square"), and **angled** (sometimes referred to as "pointed").

The **CURVED** shape reflects people-oriented causes. Among the ranks of rounded chinners are some of the world's greatest humanitarians. Round chins reveal compassion, sympathy for the problems of others, generosity, and hospitality.

Have you ever seen a picture of Laurel Robertson? She's the guiding force behind the wonderful cookbook *Laurel's Kitchen*. In keeping with her VERY **curved** chin, the book inspires the reader with friendliness and kindheartedness.

People with **STRAIGHT** chins may speak just as outspokenly for the causes they favor, but they fight for ideas and ideals. Not for people's feelings.

Does it sound abstract to imagine someone caring passionately about an idea? Just think of **straight**-chinner George Washington. Hardly an armchair philosopher! Nor was Mitch Snyder, advocate for the homeless.

As for the **ANGLED** chins, they go with an emphasis on personally taking control. No doubt such a chin helped Jim Bakker build his following as a TV evangelist. In a different way former Costa Rican president José Figueres Ferrer gained power, drawing on the strength built into his chin. Then again, you could look at Alexander Haig, Jr., the controversial hawk who rose to power as Chief of White House staff under Nixon.

My favorite activist with an **angled** chin is the Duke of Wellington, famous as the commander who defeated Napoleon at Waterloo and also as the man who brought the world Wellington boots.

Astute tennis player Jimmy Connors has used his controlling talents to win. So did legendary female athlete Babe Didrikson Zaharias.

Folks with **VERY angled** chins can be domineering. And people with **small, angled** chins have a potential challenge with impulsiveness, especially about spending money. Indeed, one psychological view interprets compulsive, impulsive spending as an attempt to take control of life. For a short time, at least, the spender feels on top of the world.

If you're looking for a chin with surprising repercussions, why not peer for a moment at an unexpected talent of Mary Pickford. As an actress, she became legendary for her winsome golden curls. But among financial experts she is recognized as the shrewdest businesswoman ever to come out of Hollywood.

CHINS PLUS EYEBROWS

As mentioned earlier, eyebrows and chins have the same three basic shapes. The significance is also the same:

- Curved for people-oriented
- Straight for idea-oriented
- Angled for control-oriented

Well, what happens when chins and eyebrows are of different shapes?

For a summary, see the accompanying Chart of Eyebrows and Chins, but the general guideline for interpretation is this:

A person will *think* and *talk* in terms symbolized by the upper part of the face; will *act* in terms symbolized by the lower, more instinctual part.

CHART OF EYEBROW AND CHIN SHAPES

Curved Eyebrows A Curved Chin	Straight Eyebrows A Curved Chin	Angled Eyebrows A Curved Chin
Puts people first, in principle and practice. •Marian Anderson •Roger Williams	Fascinated by abstract ideas. To accomplish goals, appeals to people's feelings. •Harry Truman •Johnny Cash	Skilled manipulator of ideas. Needs to shape details into a pattern that feels harmonious. •Johann Sebastian Bach •Duke of Wellington

Curved Eyebrows A Straight Chin	Straight Eyebrows A Straight Chin	Angled Eyebrows A Straight Chin
Cares about feelings and problems of people, but helps by focusing on a cause. Prefers to change the system. •Wilma Rudolph •Charles Revson	Clever at handling concepts to fulfill ideals. A persuasive communicator of ideas. •Samuel Goldwyn •David Stulberg	Creative strategist at managing ideas and people. Not shy about intimidating others with ideas and actions. •Jimmy the Greek •Jackie Robinson

Curved Eyebrows An Angled Chin	Straight Eyebrows An Angled Chin	Angled Eyebrows An Angled Chin
Notices people. Sensitive to their feelings. Stages events to profit from knowledge of how people react. •Indira Gandhi •Jane Austen	Gets involved in ideas and causes rather than people's feelings. Acts decisively, even impulsively, to further these ideas. •Billy the Kid •Babe Didrikson Zaharias	Detached from people's feelings. Skilled at carrying out set plans without being deterred from chosen purpose. •Alexander Haig •Marquis de Sade

BEARDS ARE NO MASK

Do beards make you suspicious? Do you always wonder what secret flaw the bearded one is trying to hide?

Worry no more. What you see on the outside of the face *is* the face. Therefore, beard shape is chin shape.

Any beard increases the size of the aggression and endurance areas in one hairy blast. The conscious lenghtening of the chin reflects a desire to be more dominating. This is a given. But take a look at the shape to get additional information. Is the beard trimmed off to look triangular, round, or square?

What shape of beard would you expect Santa Claus to have? A mischief-maker goatee? No way. To manage all those elves, reindeer, and materialistic kiddies, he's got to have a people-oriented curved beard.

Some men think they grow their beards to cover up a "weak" chin. But they should view it more like a transformation. What we show on our face is what we are.

So beards transform even a formerly insignificant chin into a tower of strength.

Similarly, beards transform clefts and dimples.

AH, DIMPLES

Have you wondered about the significance of clefts or dimples? Dimples show playfulness. Therefore, you can read **DIMPLES IN CHINS** as a mark of playfulness (even capriciousness) in making life decisions.

CLEFTS that divide the chin show a more extreme version— adventurousness, maybe fickleness. Multiple marriages and careers are common for folks with clefts.

Similarly, **DIMPLES IN CHEEKS** also show playfulness.

Extreme dimples are the ones that show even when the subject isn't smiling. They reveal a knack for using humor to enhance personal power. The charm can be quite calculated.

Usually, though, dimples peek out only when a subject smiles. Here the frolicsome behavior concerns romance.

An astrologer friend once told me that dimples usually coincide with prominence of Venus in a person's chart (not just the sun sign but the overall grouping of planets). Love is very important to these dimpled ones. Notice that the most convincing Cupids wear dimples.

Cheek dimples are hard to conceal—not smiling is a pretty high price to pay if you're determined to hide this form of romantic vulnerability. If you're a man, though, you could always grow a beard!

What of mustaches, then? Well, first you'll need to know all about lips. . . .

MOUTHS

Did you ever wonder why eyes, which are supposed to mirror something as intimate as the soul, get stared at most of the time, while mouths receive averted glances? Why do we tend to be so shy about staring at somebody's mouth (except to check if it is smiling)?

I think it's because staring at mouths is almost like staring at someone who is naked. More than any other facial trait, mouths reveal the physical life of your subject, including styles of sensuality and sexuality—and willingness to talk about these subjects.

WHAT YOU ALWAYS WANTED TO KNOW ABOUT LIPS BUT WERE AFRAID TO ASK

If you need a refresher course on the meaning of full lips, grab a mirror, pucker up, and get ready for a kiss. Take a good look.

Habitual **FULL** lips proclaim a person who is sensuous, emotional, and likely to be physically demonstrative. Guess how Marilyn Monroe scored at lip thickness!

Now pucker *in* your lips—as though you had just eaten a lemon. Draw your mouth into the thinnest shape you can make of it, and you'll have a sense of the opposite style.

Of course, I'm not implying that people with different lip proportions consciously stick their lips out or in. The purpose of feeling the two extremes for yourself is to alert you to the different inner modes associated with lip fullness. It takes control to cram your lips together, just as it takes uninhibitedness to balloon your lips out.

To some extent, our psychological makeup does affect lip proportion. One client, for instance, told me that her psychotherapist used to gauge progress by changes in lip fullness. During the course of therapy, Melanie went from having extremely thin lips to moderately full lips. This paralleled an opening up of self-expression.

THIN-lipped people are likely to be tight-lipped. Reserved. Without indulging as freely in the pleasures of sensuality, these folks may tend to "live in their heads."

Style of verbal expression also shows in the fullness of lips. Greater fullness relates to amount of self-disclosure. Few details are held back in conversation when lips are **extremely full.**

By contrast, the thinner the lips, the greater the reluctance to divulge personal information. Religious or spiritual beliefs, sex, even emotions may be taboo.

Nonetheless, thinner-lipped folks have a valuable strength. They are adept at small talk, and may show much greater ease at conversations that are strictly business.

LIP PROPORTION

The size and proportion of the upper and lower lip to each other is also very significant. To fathom the relative lushness of both lips, be sure to catch a subject who isn't smiling or getting ready to kiss you.

BLARNEY LIPS

Have you ever heard of the Blarney Stone? According to Irish folklore, after you kiss it you're given the gift of gab. Forever after, your speech convinces and charms the listener—no matter what you're talking about. Siang Mien expert Lailan Young gets credit for identifying a trait of lip proportion as "Blarney Lips": Just look for a lower lip at least twice as full as the upper lip.

This knowledge, alone, should be worth the price of this book. As a consumer, you'll now know to be wary when someone with these lips tries to sell you anything, be it swampland in Florida, the neatest gadget since bread slicers, or some really valuable encyclopedias.

Muster up your skepticism as soon as you eyeball those lips so that you can decide on your own. Maybe you do need another set of encyclopedias!

The reason why I recommend watching out for Blarney Lips is not that the folks who have them are necessarily dishonest. It's just that they are powerful convincers.

Here's a random assortment of people with Blarney lips from different walks of life. Some you may admire. Others you may not. All they share is lip proportions and, with them, a knack for persuasiveness.

Jerry Falwell	Evangelist
Elvis Presley	Singer
Judy Garland	Actress
Pablo Picasso	Artist
Andy Warhol	Pop art personality
Mary McFadden	Fashion designer
Brian Mulroney	Canadian prime minister
Margaret Thatcher	British prime minister
Keokuk	Tribal ruler
Carl Icahn	TWA chairman

Lip thickness

Full

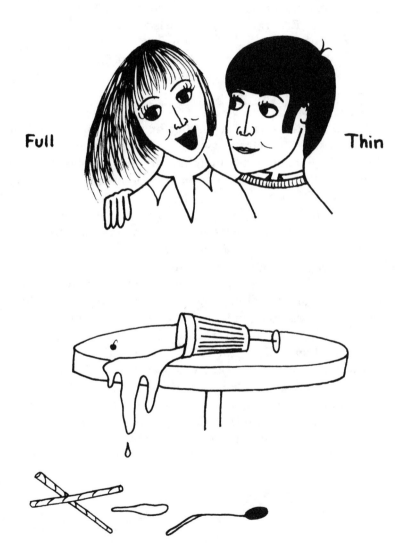

Thin

Mary Wells Lawrence	Advertising executive
Clarence Darrow	Attorney
Larry King	Radio/TV broadcaster
Craig Claiborne	Chef/Food writer
George Balanchine	Choreographer
Russell Baker	Satirist
Dave Barry*	Humorist
P. T. Barnum	Circus impresario

*No, I am not making this up.

If *you* are the one with Blarney lips, recognize the talent and find ways to make use of it. One of my students was a soft-spoken woman, definitely not dressed for success, and slumped in her chair with body language that pleaded, "Don't notice me."

Julie's chin was markedly lacking in aggression. Her cheekbones were invisible. Yet when class members compared lips, we discovered that she was the only one with a built-in gift of the gab. Well, did Julie's face light up.

"That's it!" she shouted. "I never understood it before. I took a test for sales ability once and beat out everyone. They said I was by far the most persuasive. I even scored higher than two *men* who had worked in sales for *years* and taken all kinds of *special training*. Figure that out!"

Now I won't claim this elderly housewife marched forth and conquered a million-dollar sales account the next day. Something did happen to her self-confidence, though. You could hear it in her voice. Julie works as a political advocate for the homeless, and I'll bet they're more grateful than ever now for her services.

Special lip talents

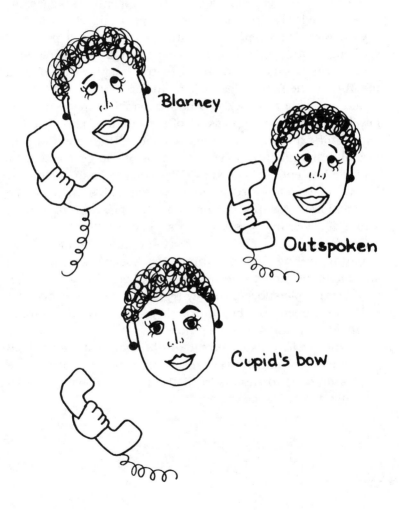

Blarney

Outspoken

Cupid's bow

LAURA'S THEORY OF LIPNESS

When you start looking for Blarney lips, you may also find many examples of people with just the opposite trait. Instead of a lower lip bigger than average, their upper lip is bigger—as wide as the lower lip. That's a lot of upper lip!

Outspoken lips represent a strength but also a potential challenge. Often others don't trust what these people say, even if the words are identical to the language used by a member of the Blarney gang. Why the credibility problem?

Like all facial features, lips have a symbolic meaning. The lower lip stands for expression of masculine energy; the upper lip for expression of feminine energy. Regardless of gender, all human beings have both kinds of energy available.

Masculine energy is good at *doing*—accomplishing things. In our male-dominated society, we trust this. When male energy dominates in self-expression, by showing the world a king-size lower lip, persuasiveness comes easily.

Feminine energy has a different specialty, *being*—understanding, feeling, and imagining. As a society, we tend to be suspicious of people who talk readily about this side of life. So when people subconsciously register the significance of a generous upper lip, they brace themselves. What personal comment is going to come up now?

On the positive side, **outspoken** lips suggest exceptional perceptiveness and the courage to express the truth. Once the lesson of gentleness is learned, the challenge with credibility tends to disappear.

THE SECRET OF MUSTACHES

The important thing about mustaches, for face reading, concerns whether or not they cover up the upper lip.

When a mustache hides the lip, the man is symbolically negating his capacity to express feelings. He wants to show the world a totally masculine image. No feminine energies of the upper lip for him!

Robert Duvall's occasional mustache, for instance, has helped him to play the strong, silent type. Another champion of the rugged mustached type is actor Tom Selleck.

A completely different kind of mustache can frame the upper lip, in effect extending it. These are on the men who express feelings more readily than the men with no mustaches at all. As an extreme (and negative) example, think of the emotionalism of Adolf Hitler.

Frequently, you'll find that "sensitive men" (the kind who'll admit to thriving on quiche and growth seminars) sport this kind of mustache.

THE TALENT FOR MANIFESTATION

CUPID'S BOW lips also show a predilection for expressing feminine energy. When you see those well-defined upper lips with triangles at the center, know that you are in the presence of someone with a wonderful gift:

More easily than others, they say what they want and they get it.

You'll notice these lips on some entertainers who have helped to crystallize social movements to match their beliefs: Joan Baez and Shirley MacLaine.

But women aren't the only ones to express the talent for manifestation through well-defined upper lips. Developer Donald Trump has managed to materialize his desires in a big way.

Satchel Paige actualized the career he wanted in baseball, despite the odds against it. And perhaps the upper lip of Yuri Gagarin is what helped him to realize the dream of any red-blooded earthling, to be picked as the first cosmonaut to orbit in space.

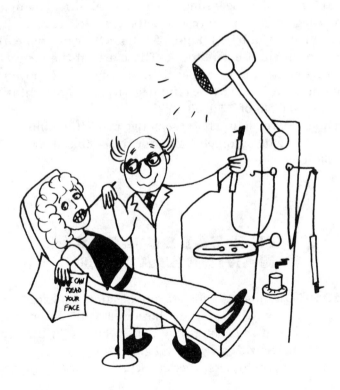

DO BIG MOUTHS HAVE MORE FUN?

It's true. People whose mouths are generously proportioned do seem to have more fun socially. They talk more. They express themselves more—even before total strangers.

To pick one of these life-of-the-party types, go by two traits. First comes lip thickness, second is overall length of the mouth in proportion to nose tip and eyes.

Long mouths with **full** lips count as officially **BIG** mouths. The entertainment business rewards their typically wacky humor. (Could mouth size explain how these celebrities manage to swallow the little fish who try to compete for the laughs?)

Mouth proportion in face

Big   Short   Long

Honestly, could you imagine David Letterman, Art Buchwald, Lily Tomlin, or Carol Burnett with shy, reserved little mouths?

Woody Allen has a small mouth, sure, but his comedy persona isn't an outgoing Rodney Dangerfield kind of guy. He bottles up feelings inside, nurses old insults, and broods over the words that come out of his mouth. "Should I have said that or shouldn't I?" That's the challenge built into a **short** mouth, along with fear of public speaking.

The gift of a **short** mouth is sincerity. These people excel at one-on-one conversations.

A variation on the **big** mouth is the large mouth that is simply **LONG.** The lips are not full.

People with such mouths, on the whole, do not have as outrageous a sense of humor as those with the **long, full** mouths. They excel at public speaking, or any kind of talking to people that does *not* involve divulging deeply personal information.

READ HIS LIPS

The message behind the lips of George Bush—or anyone—is personal style of self-expression. Though, of course, Bush speaks to others with ease, I'll bet that even at home he's reticent about divulging his deep feelings and beliefs.

What kind of humor do you expect from his kind of **LONG, THIN** mouth? Wry. Have you ever read a newspaper column by Mike Royko? His wisecracks are scathing—and hilarious.

Garrison Keillor, another humorist with a **long, thin** mouth, turns his attention to other locales, notably Lake Wobegon. He also has taken on important social causes, including the perfect one for a man with thin lips, "Shy Rights."

When you combine a **MODERATE**ly long mouth with **thin** lips, you typically get the teasing kind of humor for which Johnny Carson has become legendary.

Mouth puckers

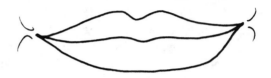

SHORT mouths with **thin** lips are the **SMALL** mouths. They go with the greatest reserve. Suspicion can be a challenge as well. These are the people *not* to compliment until you know them well. A rapport must be established over time.

Having a **small** versus a **big** mouth does not necessarily mean that someone is insecure rather than confident. But mouth size does show quite reliably the style with which a person uses however much confidence is available.

So where do you read confidence about self-expression? Occasionally you may see little **PUCKERS** at the corners of someone's lips (and not when that someone is smiling or playing the oboe—when lips are relaxed). Look at those indentations as microphones to broadcast a message of . . . insecurity.

Here is someone who does not dare to speak the whole truth. Tune in to that person's past and you'll probably hear harsh words of criticism or scolding. These people may feel ashamed to speak at all, as though they were obnoxious. Whether or not they really are, your acceptance will encourage folks with "hold back" lips to relax and speak freely.

And one final Face Reading Secret about lips: Study texture.

SMOOTH texture bespeaks a more emotionally carefree life. Deeply wrinkled or **ROUGH** lips reveal the pain of limited opportunity for self-expression.

HOW ABOUT TEETH?

Teeth symbolize major life decisions. They relate to the ability to break down ideas, analyze them, and make choices.

Siang Mien notes that people with evenly spaced, straight teeth learn life lessons quickly. In other words, they make decisions wisely. Therefore, the teeth go with a sense of being capable.

EVEN teeth help Oprah Winfrey maintain her poise as a TV talk show hostess, no matter how outrageous the conversations she precipitates with that large mouth.

GAPS in the spacing of teeth represent gaps in the logic of decision making. (Perhaps gaps like these affected the choice of words for Hall of Famer Yogi Berra, who developed a unique style of eloquence.) The gaps go with an intuitive style of decision making. People with these teeth can handle taking risks—emotional, financial, or athletic.

When you see that the two front teeth are **BIG** compared to the others, you're looking at a valuable asset for personal achievement: stubbornness. Once such people make a decision, that's that! Another baseball star, Joe DiMaggio, may have depended on stubbornness for his staying power as a hitter.

TINY front teeth, no larger than the others, suggest the opposite trait, a lack of personal boundaries. Selflessness is the positive side, conflict about pushiness is the possible challenge.

A rare but fascinating trait is **LARGE** canine teeth that are longer than the front teeth. When those pointy, fanglike teeth dominate, beware of exceptional aggression. These folks go after what they want tooth and nail.

As for **CROOKED** teeth, which grow at angles to each other, this symbolizes conflict about major life choices.

Sometimes you'll meet an especially shy person who struggles to be outgoing, bending over backward in the quest for popularity. Chances are, this goes with an **overbite**. The extreme version is **BUCK** teeth.

A rarer trait is the opposite, an **underbite** (where the lower set of teeth stick out farther than the upper teeth). A noticeable underbite is the deepest sign of aggression you can find in a face, often associated with grimness or bitterness.

Everyday language supports the symbolism linking teeth with determination. We use expressions like *sink one's teeth into* to mean getting actively involved and *show one's teeth* for a readiness to fight.

No wonder people feel so helpless when their teeth get pulled. But here's good news for denture wearers. From the standpoint of Face Reading Secrets, "false" teeth are fully as good as originals.

That goes for fillings, caps, and all the amazing cosmetic feats of dentistry. When dentists talk about "restorations," they may inadvertently be speaking of inner characteristics as well.

OPTIMISM INDEX

There are times when it helps to know whether a person is an Optimist.

When was the last time you came up with a creative new idea? Following through on creative ideas involves sharing them with other people. The last person you should pick to meet your tender newborn brainchild is a Pessimist. At this stage nurturing is needed, so haul an Optimist onto the scene.

(Later on, sure, get input from a Pessimist or Realist— especially if you're a rampant Optimist about to make an expensive commitment.)

Reading optimism, both in yourself and in others, will improve your ability to evaluate what you hear and anticipate the reactions of others. Your business and social dealings may benefit if you decide to balance your relative pessimism with optimism, or your optimism with realism.

Now, I can't claim that my Optimism Index is entirely a new discovery. Back in 1896, Charles Darwin noticed that laughter goes with upward slanting mouth corners, while depression correlates with lips and eyebrows that droop. Siang Mien masters have been at it much longer.

My contribution was to put together the two main ways to gauge optimism and clarify their relationship.

ACTION

The first part of the Optimism Index shows in **EYE ANGLE.** Most people do not know how to recognize this, confusing it with eye shape. Here's how to tell:

Focus on the inner and outer corners of your subject's right eye (or use the left one, if you prefer). Imagine dots in each corner. Now draw a mental line from the inner dot, next to the nose, to the outer dot. This version of "Connect the dots" gives you an angle.

Does the angle go up (that's the direction of Spock's eyebrows in *Star Trek*)? Do the eyes angle down, like actor Sylvester Stallone's? Or are the eyes straight? The interpretation is:

- Up for Optimism
- Down for Pessimism
- Straight for Realism

This first half of the Optimism Index shows how your subject views life in general. I call it the Action part of the Index because overall view of life affects which actions people choose.

Optimists are the most willing to act on the basis of creative imagination. Furthermore, the more the angle is **VERY upward,** the more idealistic the vision of life. They see what can go right, not what can go wrong.

The potential challenges are proportional to the risks these people take. "Look before you leap" was probably coined by the parents of some irrepressible optimist.

Famous Optimists include Helen Keller, who smashed the

Eye angle

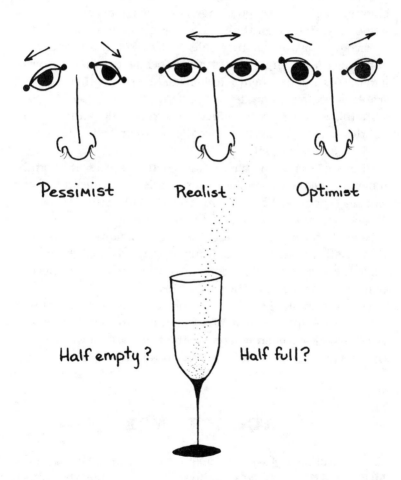

Pessimist   Realist   Optimist

Half empty ?   Half full?

world's preconceptions about what a disabled person could accomplish; actor Tom Hanks, who broke through the time barrier in his magnificent performance in *Big*; and as you'd expect if you thought about it, Napoleon Bonaparte, one-time aspirant for the title of World Emperor.

Pessimists are the least likely to tear off on wild-goose chases. In fact, their challenge is to let opportunities go by while they analyze all the things that could go wrong.

Recognizing the seamier side of life is both strength and challenge. More than others, these people can handle problems. This makes them excellent listeners to other people's troubles—compassionate and patient.

In the arts they are valued for expressing suffering. In politics, they are survivors because of their ability to handle challenge and conflict.

Built-in Pessimism has enhanced the careers of sculptor Alberto Giacometti; satirist Ambrose Bierce; Speaker of the House, Democrat Sam Rayburn; historian Arthur M. Schlesinger, Jr.; and King Faisal of Saudi Arabia.

Realists have the special gift of fairness. More than others, they see things as they are. Emily Post helped her generation walk the straight-and-narrow path of etiquette. She needed realism—and tact, another gift of Realists.

The only challenge these folks need to watch out for is lack of tolerance for the rest of humanity. The Optimists and Pessimists have good reason for their ups and downs, even if they seem a bit extreme to a dyed-in-the-wool Realist.

ACCEPTANCE

The second part of the Optimism Index, which shows in the **MOUTH ANGLE,** refers to how people handle the consequences of their actions. Especially, how do they accept the things others say about them?

Mouth angle

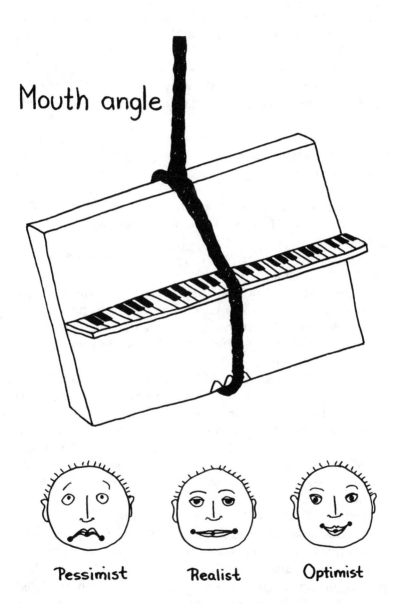

Pessimist   Realist   Optimist

Examine the mouth in repose. Imagine dots again: one at each mouth corner and one at the center of the mouth, where the lips meet. Connect the dots to get two lines, one for each side of the face.

Read each side of the mouth separately. Does the angle tilt up at the corners, sag down, or go straight? Once again, read:

- Up for Optimism
- Down for Pessimism
- Straight for Realism

Say your subject walks down the street. An acquaintance comes into view. He says, "I'm in a terrible rush. Can't stop to talk, sorry."

A Realist might react: "What's going on with him? Wonder why he's in such a rush."

By contrast, an Optimist might react: "He was sorry he couldn't talk to me—how nice of him to explain he was in a hurry. He's probably rushing to put a lot of money in the bank or something like that. Seems like he's been on a winning streak lately."

A Pessimist's version would be different: "What a coldness in his voice—and to think we used to be friends. Reminds me of the time Hubert did the same thing."

You see, Pessimists interpret comments to mean the worst. The challenge is obvious. The strength is that these people are highly sensitive to hurting people's feelings through hasty speech—they know all too well how it feels like to be on the receiving end.

Most people fit into the **Pessimist** category.

The **Optimists** don't hold grudges about what people say. Left-handed compliments may be accepted at face value.

Actor Ted Danson has this kind of mouth, making him perfect for the rough joking in *Cheers*. In fact, the challenge with optimistic lips is too much joking. These folks may not realize how hurtful it can be to oversensitive types.

As for the rare Realists, they sort through the statement to hear what it literally says. Others may find this style cold or unimaginative, but it's probably the most stable of the three.

Lucille Ball used the perspective of a Realist mouth to create the classic sitcom of *I Love Lucy*.

One very interesting face, in terms of the Optimism Index, belongs to Dr. Norman Vincent Peale. He has eyes and lips that point down on the right side of his face, point up on the left.

My interpretation is that he has had a major life challenge to transform a negative attitude into a positive one; mastering this life lesson prepared him to become the world's foremost positive thinker.

LIFE PRIORITIES

THE FOCUS OF A FACE

If you think about people you know well, they tend to be expressive with different parts of their faces. One friend may wrinkle her forehead a lot. Another may crinkle up his nose. Yet another may register every passing emotion by moving her mouth.

That's expression, telling you something about which area of life people put their energy into. Well, Priority Areas reveal something related. Which areas of life, symbolized by facial proportions, matter most to your subject?

PRIORITY AREA 1 reaches from the hairline to the highest part of the eyebrows (*the forehead area*).

PRIORITY AREA 2 goes from the highest point of the eyebrows to the bottom of the nose, either nostrils or nose tip, choosing whichever is lower (*eyes and nose*).

PRIORITY AREA 3 extends from the overlip (the area of flesh between nose and mouth) to the chin (*lips and chin*).

Some faces emphasize forehead. Others are mostly nose or chin. We're apt to think of these proportions as an accident, purely heredity. Well, it may be heredity but I can assure you, it's also significant.

YOU DON'T NEED A RULER

What's the best way to measure these Priority Areas? Try the two-finger method.

Span the distance from hairline to eyebrow with your thumb and forefinger. That's Priority Area 1, remember. Hold these two fingers in place. Freeze! There's your measuring stick.

Now, move your thumb and forefinger to Priority Area 2. Is it bigger or smaller? How about Priority Area 3?

If 2 or 3 is bigger than 1, span that distance with thumb and forefinger to make a new measuring stick. Use that measure to compare to the smaller regions.

Remember, the measurements don't have to be precise. Your goal is an intuitive sizing up of proportion.

THOSE EMBARRASSING AREAS

Bald heads and double chins can be great sources of embarrassment to their owners. They can also be a minor embarrassment to the novice face reader who isn't sure whether or not to count them.

The answer is no.

Should your subject have no hair left to form a hairline, imagine where it would be. Should your subject have two or three chins, count only the first one.

When you interpret the face overall, however, remember that baldness signifies a lot of thinking and worrying. Extra chins reveal intense interest in life's creature comforts. These are important points to make when you do a Reading. Another one is this:

"You're not getting older. You're getting better."

A face should change as a person matures—reflecting life lessons learned.

LIFE PRIORITY 1: THINKING

People who have Priority 1 as their **LARGEST** area are Thinkers. They are bullish on abstract ideas, imagination, theories, and planning. Expect them to excel at occupations like science, philosophy, academics, and writing.

Some famous people who are Thinkers are Pope John Paul II (of the aforementioned wonderful nose roots), Supreme Court Justice Sandra Day O'Connor, composer Walter Piston, physicist Dr. Enrico Fermi, naturalist Jean Louis Agassiz, linguist Dr. Noam Chomsky, and psychologist Dr. Carl Rogers.

Thinkers adore long words and long sentences. They find a fascination with fine distinctions that could (and, when tested, do) bore others stiff.

So if *you* have a prominent Area 1, be aware that not everyone else does. You'll win a wider variety of friends if you can bring yourself to cut some of those long stories short.

People with a **VERY SMALL** Area 1 have just the opposite challenge. These folks don't get criticized for being too subtle. They go after what they want like gangbusters. "Battling Bella" Abzug and political activist Cesar Chavez are two wonderful examples.

LIFE PRIORITY 2: AMBITION

Priority Area 2 represents action. People who fill up most of their facial real estate with a **Big** Area 2 are unabashed go-getters. They care about money, status, prestige, and *owning* the best. (By contrast, Area 3 people care about *enjoying* the best—savoring creature comforts.)

Ever hear of Tom Hopkins? He has been described as the nation's top sales trainer. Another Ambition face, Joe Girard, made the *Guinness Book of World Records* as the World's

Priority examples

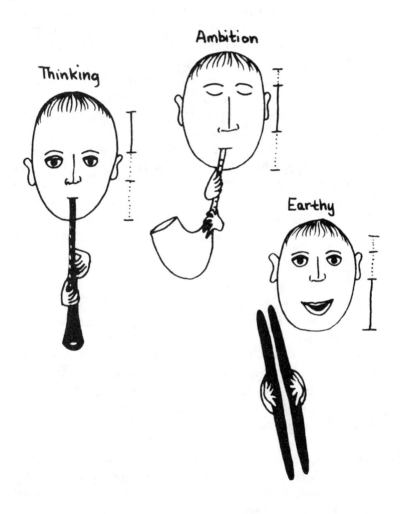

Greatest Salesman. Selling can be a great occupation for Area 2 people.

Ambition people may be just as intelligent as the Thinkers, but their emphasis is different. Once they understand something in theory, they yearn and burn to do something with it.

Once Henry Ford understood how the assembly line could be used to manufacture cars, he capitalized on it. Remember his famous line about Model T's, "Pick any color you want, so long as it's black"? That's a perfect action-oriented answer.

Since the days of the Model T, technology has kept driving ahead, and folks with a big Area 2 keep moving up in the fast lane. A present-day example is Nam June Paik, a video art innovator famous for his "action concerts."

Historically, action people George and Martha Washington worked to shape the emerging American nation. Alexander the Great was not timid about trying to leave his mark on the world, either.

Nor is political power the only attractive commodity for these movers and shakers. Tennis player John McEnroe has made ambition profitable too.

Influential TV interviewer Barbara Walters has made no secret of her drive to succeed. "I got to where I am," she once said, "by hard work and perseverance."

Now, it would be misleading to give the impression that all Ambitious people aspire to be famous. Their ambitions may extend no farther than relish for life's everyday activities. One of the most famous diarists of Western culture was Samuel Pepys, who faithfully noted his everyday comings and goings. Indeed, Area 2 people tend to be exceptionally proud of all their varied accomplishments.

When you speak to Ambition people, you'll rivet their attention with shorter words, verbs rather than adjectives, action instead of description. Most important is pace. Get to the point.

If *you* have a prominent Area 2, your challenge is patience. Remember personal patience—your drive to accomplish can be satisfied even if you give yourself some playtime. Even more important, cultivate patience with others, who may seem exasperatingly slow at getting things done compared with you.

A challenge for a **VERY SMALL** Area 2 might be not profiting financially from your actions. You're likely to wind up more respected than wealthy, like the Nobel prize–winners Aleksandr Solzhenitsyn and Ilya Prigogine.

LIFE PRIORITY 3: EARTHINESS

People with a **BIG** Area 3 excel at getting down to earth. Presented with new ideas, they prefer *sharing* their reactions to ideas with friends. They may also pace around, because for them learning doesn't just take place in the head; it's a whole-body activity.

Their being street smart is part of the gift. They check in with reality more often than others—see what other people are doing, not just assuming things based on fantasy.

Sex may be a very important form of communication for them, and they're likely to think about it more than people with predominant Areas 1 or 2.

Remember, the Life Priority perspective is about people's built-in comfort zones and personal style. As an Earthy person, you may be brilliant at understanding and accomplishing. The difference is, you don't need to spend as much time dwelling on this as folks with the other kinds of faces. And whatever you think about, you take that extra step to bring it down to earth.

This fits in perfectly with the earthy emphasis of U.S. culture. The all-American look we find appealing often comes from predominant Area 3's—Christie Brinkley today, Lauren Bacall more famous a generation ago but still going strong. This face proportion isn't the most common one around, but you will find it well represented in fashion magazines and on the sports pages.

Wherever we see the Earthy faces, we tend to trust them.

When they talk, what makes the impression isn't so much the words chosen as the sense of being physically integrated. Earthy people are connected to their bodies. They don't come across as talking heads.

No wonder they can excel as politicians, social workers, farmers, mechanics, and athletes. It's rare to find a professional baseball player who *doesn't* have a large Priority Area 3.

Hugh Hefner has made a career out of appealing to earthier instincts. In a different way, so did playwright Tennessee Williams. And how about Mae West, famous for her earthy humor!

Actress turned exercise guru Jane Fonda has rehabilitated countless couch potatoes. Advice columnists Ann Landers and Abigail Van Buren use their down-to-earth viewpoints to help readers "Wake up and smell the coffee."

Many of our longtime popular entertainers have been Earthies—like Frank Sinatra, Dean Martin, and the late Sammy Davis, Jr.

If *you* are Earthy, recognize that you have the advantage of being tougher than others. Your feelings are hurt less easily. You feel safer showing enthusiasm. Realize, too, that others may be more reserved than you or may need to stay in their heads more often.

The more respect you can show for them, the more they'll respect you.

As for faces with a **VERY SMALL** Area 3, they may reveal talents but won't include an instinctive fascination with physical grounding. Indeed, compensating for this lack can become part of their life's work. Christian Science founder Mary Baker Eddy was an example.

Generations of English students have read William Wordsworth's "Lines composed a few miles above Tintern Abbey." The poem is brilliant and inspiring, etc. On the other hand, quite possibly he wrote it while getting lost . . . on the way to Tintern Abbey. The man was definitely a great poet, but I wouldn't have trusted him to draw a decent map.

(If you ever get a chance to see a picture of Wordsworth, take a good look. He had a prodigious forehead and magnificent Stradivarius-style nose, but not much chin.)

Jules Feiffer, the great cartoonist, has expressed perfectly how much fascination with physical grounding is typical for a person with very small Area 3: "One of my great desires to grow up was that, as I understood it, adults did not have to take gym."

COMBINATIONS

So far you've had a chance to view the three types where one Life Priority dominates a face. More commonly, two areas are close in size. This is what we'll look at next.

When **AREAS 1 and 2 TIE** in size, or 1 is just slightly larger, expect to find someone who is driven to find new ideas and make them work in a practical way.

That's a powerful combination for innovative business, as in the case of Harvey Firestone, who set up the Firestone Tire & Rubber Co. Or Dr. An Wang, founder of Wang Laboratories. Harold Geneen, as president of the International Telephone and Telegraph Company, kept expanding the scope of operations and building financial profits.

When **AREAS 1 and 3 TIE,** or 1 is just slightly larger, expect imagination to be expressed in a down-to-earth way. James Underwood Crockett has grounded his ideas quite literally—as a gardener.

When **AREAS 3 and 1 TIE,** or 3 is just slightly larger, expect to find a thoughtful person who savors physical pleasures. Jeff Smith, The Frugal Gourmet, is one example. Another is Robert Frost, who could write about a road not taken and put deep symbolic value into an everyday experience.

When **AREAS 2 and 3 TIE,** or 2 is just slightly larger, expect to find someone who works hard but keeps more connected to others than clear Priority Area 2 people. The ability to integrate physically what they understand gives them strong credibility on a gut level.

Thus, Dr. Martin Luther King, Jr., didn't just have a dream. He marched it into action and helped people feel it in an unforgettable way. Maya Angelou's writings have communicated her ability to survive—from the gut and the heart, not the realm of theory.

Julia Child, like many other professionals in the food industry, is strong in the grounding of Area 3. It's interesting to contrast her 2 and 3 style to that of the aforementioned 3 and 1 chef Jeff Smith. Julia's a whirlwind of activity. Jeff is a torrent of conversation.

I imagine that a meal at his house would last about twice as long. *Chez* Julia, you'd savor the food at least as much, but briskly, and then everyone would jump up and *do* something, like go out to a concert.

Finally, come the cases where Areas 1, 2, and 3 show up in more or less **EQUAL** proportions. This rare balance can be reflected in many wonderful attributes.

These people find it relatively easy to balance the different concerns in life—family, health, career, religion. As leaders they have outstanding ability to communicate with people with any Life Priorities.

Folks who have capitalized on their strengths as Balanced Priority people include psychologist Erik Erikson (whose discoveries are the bible for contemporary social work training); influential merchandiser A. Montgomery Ward; social forecaster John Naisbitt; U.S. Senator Daniel Inouye; and Dr. Benjamin Spock, the child-care expert whose views on balanced upbringing have affected the lives of millions of baby boomers.

Soviet leader Mikhail Gorbachev has balanced Priority Areas. In addition, his power structures of cheeks, chin, and nose are in perfect proportion. Good choice to send to a peace summit!

CHART OF PRIORITY AREAS

Here is a summary of the significance of all three Priority Areas, in different combinations, and the strengths that go with them. Examples are provided for each case.

1: INTELLECTUAL 1 Biggest	2: AMBITIOUS 2 Biggest	3: EARTHY 3 Biggest
Thinking, planning, teaching. Original ideas. •Pope John Paul II	Getting things done, making money. •Tom Hopkins	Communicating feelings physically. •Hugh Hefner

1 Biggest, 2 Second or Equal	2 Biggest, 3 Second or Equal	3 Biggest, 1 Second or Equal
Making new ideas work in a practical way. •Harvey Firestone	Leading others, respected as down to earth. •Dr. Martin Luther King, Jr.	Aware of environment, imaginative. •Robert Frost

1 Biggest, 3 Second or Equal	2 Biggest, 1 Second or Equal	3 Biggest 2 Second or Equal
Thoughtful, down to earth. •James Underwood Crockett	Focusing on goals, still experiments with many new theories. •Harold Geneen	Creative finder of practical uses for available resources. •Maya Angelou

Areas 1, 2, and 3 of Equal Size

Balances personal life-style: family, health, career, religion. Popular—has credibility with people representing all the Priority Area combinations noted above. •Mikhail Gorbachev

MISCELLANEOUS TRAITS

WRINKLES

WRINKLES testify to worldly experience. They also emphasize that the subject frequently uses that part of the face! Read them as if a highlighter pen were underscoring words on a page: *Wrinkles make features stand out.* Here are interpretations for the most common ones:

Read laugh lines as a widening out of the lips. Interpret them as you do long mouths.

Frown lines curve down to accentuate oversensitivity.

Burnout lines cross the bridge of the nose, suggesting intense commitment to work . . . and the challenge of not being able physically to handle a workaholic life-style.

Deep lines from nose to mouth mark a great deal of suffering (whether directly or through empathy for others).

Wrinkles over the cheeks show there has been great need for courage.

Wrinkles around eyes show effort to see. If they're greatest at the side of the eyes, read them as perspective. If the lines show more under the eyes, read them as openness to others.

Perpendicular forehead furrows suggest efforts to concentrate.

SPECIAL MARKS

BIRTHMARKS, **WARTS**, and **MOLES** are signals to pay attention to the part of the face where they are located. Something needs to be noticed. It may be a special challenge or a special ability.

The large red birthmark on Gorbachev's forehead is a reminder of this man's exceptionally brilliant mind.

PIMPLES represent temporary challenges. Once I met a multimillionaire's son who had a large pimple on his nose tip—and who was feeling irritated at the pressures of wealth.

RIGHT AND LEFT SIDES

When you interpret faces with mixed sides, the simplest interpretation is: The subject has both X and Y. This adds up to double the strengths, double the potential challenges. You'll see an example of this in my reading of Eddie Murphy.

A more sophisticated interpretation involves the symbology of the sides of the face.

The right side relates to action in the world. You can read it as the public version of your subject's personality.

The left side relates to inner reactions to experience. Interpret this as the private personality, what your subject really feels and thinks, deep down. You'll see an example of this kind of interpretation in my reading of Albert Einstein.

NOSE PROMINENCE

The more a nose sticks out from the head, the more your subject desires to be influential through work. Career aspirations of someone with a flatter nose show more of a homebody style.

So read nose prominence to get a sense of your subject's ambitions to expand his territory of influence. Would he rather get rich having his work seen by six people or by six thousand?

EAR CIRCLES

When you look at an ear closely, you'll notice that it includes an inner circle, an outer circle, a border between these two circles, and a lobe.

Proportions of inner and outer circles signify how much your subject pays attention to subjective versus objective experiences in life. Do feelings dominate or facts?

Typically, Americans have elected presidents whose outer circles predominate. This makes sense, since folks with huge inner circles are the potential bleeding hearts, deeply sensitive people. Bigger outer circles denote a practical focus.

Our only president so far with larger inner circles than outer was Franklin Delano Roosevelt.

The border (which admittedly takes practice to read) is also significant. A well-defined border is like a psychological sign that reads NO TRESPASSING. Your subject can easily distinguish subjective from objective reality. Even if she's terribly upset about something, she can drop it to go into a business meeting.

By contrast, mushy or incomplete borders suggest leakage between subjectivity and objectivity. The worst case is

Ear circle sizes

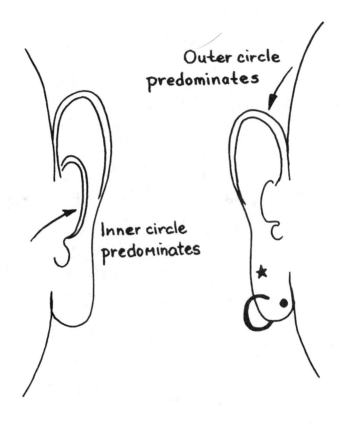

Outer circle predominates

Inner circle predominates

oversubjectivity, where a subject constantly projects his emotions onto the facts without knowing he does it.

The best case is unflagging integrity, where a subject insists on carrying ethical or spiritual beliefs into every facet of experience, rather than the more usual tendency to compartmentalize them and bring them out when convenient.

Borders of inner ear circles:

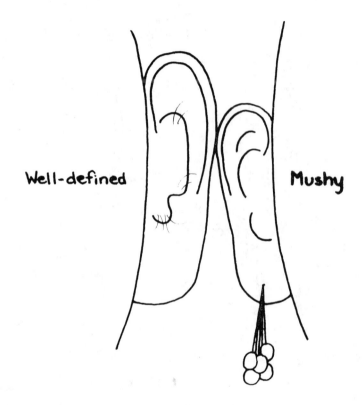

Well-defined   Mushy

EARLOBES

Earlobes symbolize awareness of the physical aspects of life.
Folks with extra large earlobes aren't only aware of how
people dress—they notice whether or not the clothes fit the
body.

OVERLIP

The space between the nose and upper lip is a part of the face you're most likely to notice if you're a man and you have to shave it. I call this area the "overlip." See the two vertical lines I'm talking about?

The more defined they are, the greater your subject's fascination with the difference between masculine and feminine: sex roles reflected in dress, speech, and behavior. The mushier the lines on the overlip, the more your subject lives in a unisex world.

We're talking about awareness of sex here, you see, not how often or how skillfully someone performs sexual acts.

CHIN CIRCLES

Occasionally you will notice a chin that has a prominent half circle of flesh, defined by a line over it. Tom Selleck and Ted Danson both have this trait. The significance is a fierce attachment to sexual identity. Challenge their masculinity and they will get extremely angry.

AM I SEXY?

The secrets revealed by the face won't give you a yes or no answer, but they will inform you about sexual style.

Sheer fascination with things physical shows in a broad chin like sexologist Dr. Ruth Westheimer. A large Priority Area 3 is also related to reveling in purely physical charms.

Emotional openness is an important facet of sexual style. It shows in the size and depth of inner ear circles, the amount of curve in the Wariness Index, and eyelid thickness.

Spontaneous demonstrativeness is another indicator of how someone expresses passion. Spontaneity lurks in a small, pointed chin; a ski jump nose; upturned nose tip; and dimples.

BEAUTY AND UGLINESS

Dazzling good looks are a gift—and also a challenge because you get extra attention, like it or not. Exceptional ugliness or physical deformity likewise bring extra attention. Learning to handle being stared at can motivate people to evolve spiritually.

As a face reader, what you want to do is question what about the face is so attractive or repellent.

If one feature is excessively large or small, interpret it as a VERY.

Many of the facial traits we are programmed to consider most beautiful may be exasperating to live with. For instance, an Elizabeth Taylorish, delicate chin may go with oversensitivity to criticism, impulsive decisions, and fickleness.

For any man who has been programmed to value a date's attractiveness as a measure of his worth or status, the "perfect romance" may remain a fantasy. Why? The behavior traits that would make his fantasy worth living quite simply may not come with the faces he has been programmed to judge desirable.

Cher's gaunt cheeks may be gorgeous, but how easy do you think they are to live with?

If you would like to raise your consciousness about potential dates, here's how to use Face Reading Secrets to reprogram yourself. Reread this book, underlining the behavior traits that make you feel good, rather than the facial traits you've been told you need. Make a new list of some of the features you'd like to have a relationship with, and don't be ashamed if they include traits like big ears, chubby cheeks, and broad chins.

USING FACE READING SECRETS IN REAL LIFE

QUICKIE READINGS

For first impressions, nothing beats a face-reading quickie. One man I know claims he can screen any potential date within three minutes. Whether your motives in wanting to assess people relate to business or pleasure, you can glean the most vital information.

- Need to know how someone follows through on details? Go for distribution of hair on eyebrows. Then check Life Priorities to assess which matters more, theory or action.
- To assess your date's relative interest in jogging versus reading, eyeball the size of Priority Areas 3 and 1.

- Before throwing out compliments to someone you want to impress, check out the mouth (unless it happens to be on a gift horse). The owner of a small mouth is more reserved, especially if lips are thin. Deep-set eyes mean she's even more reserved. If, in addition, ears lie close to her head, hold off on that compliment until she knows you very well.
- Is power your game? Then give a once-over to every player's setup of cheeks, chin, and nose.
- To quickly tune in to an old or new friend's wavelength, check for eyebrow shape and choose your conversation accordingly. (It also helps to mirror your subject's body language—for instance, hold your arms and legs in positions similar to your friend's.)
- As for those quick dating decisions, you might choose someone with Life Priorities and nostril shape similar to your own. At least you'll have similar attention spans for different activities . . . and be comfortable with how much gets spent on them.

READING DEEP

Speaking of new dates, to get to know anyone better, why not offer to do a face reading? How refreshingly humble compared to the old line "Haven't I seen you somewhere before?" Here's a chance to meet someone in the present and offer a gift few folks will refuse.

Years later, people still thank me for the Face Reading Secrets I told them. It's easy to understand why. Just think back to your own experience and remember the people who helped you the most. Weren't they the ones who could appreciate the special things about you?

Here are some practical tips to get started on doing a complete reading. Get a commitment of fifteen minutes or longer from your subject. (Mine take a whole hour, but you don't need to start off with that much detail.)

Since the secrets you discuss can be extremely personal, I'd recommend that you do the reading in private. Even at a busy party, you can step into a hallway where other people won't be able to eavesdrop. Remember, don't try to flatter people. Simply read with respect.

Your first full reading should, of course, be your own face. Satisfy that curiosity at last! After all, when you see a group picture that includes yourself, whom do you look for first?

Another advantage of reading yourself for starters is that you'll appreciate what it feels like to be on the receiving end. Remember, other people will feel at least as vulnerable when you read them. Train yourself to honor their trust so that the secrets you reveal will be helpful.

Remember *the biggest secret of Face Reading Secrets:* Treat each subject like the most important person in the world. This will help you find a way in to that face.

Now turn to the "Quick Checklist for Face Reading Secrets" at the back of the book. Go through the face trait by trait.

For best results, keep these guidelines in mind:

INTERPRETATION GUIDELINES

1. Set some sort of positive intention at the start of each reading, at least to yourself and even better, aloud to your subject. Try something like this: "I would like to help you to understand yourself better, appreciate yourself more, and use your talents in life most fully."

    Both you and your subject will become more open and receptive to helpful information.

2. With each trait, say what you see physically and then explain what it means: for example, "I can tell by the angle of your ears that you're a big nonconformist."

3. In your interpretation, remember that VERY = VERY. Extreme features parallel strong characteristics. More moderate features show traits to a lesser extent.

4. Remember that the strengths in faces are automatically mirrored by inner talents. Challenges are possibilities, not inevitabilities. If you do comment on potential challenges, mention them along with the corresponding strengths.

5. Should you miss something along the way and notice it later on in your reading, go ahead and mention it when it comes up. Intuition matters more than hitting every point in order. As an experienced reader, you will tend to notice related characteristics simultaneously and hardly go by the list at all.

6. How do you handle seeming contradictions on a face? Don't avoid them. Use intuition to resolve them.

7. Ask questions. Verification builds confidence. The nuances brought out by your subject can help you to gain more understanding as a basis for reading the rest of the face.

ACCURACY

You may be amazed at the words that come out of your mouth sometimes, but check with people afterward. "Is that so?" With repeated validation, you'll *really* be amazed.

What if many people consistently tell you, "No, not true"?

Clearly, you're not just dealing with one subject's resistance. This is a message to fine-tune your intuition.

My experience in teaching has shown one of the following is usually happening:

• Lack of experience at reading faces. (Intelligent practice makes perfect. So keep reading and learning the best that you can. Your accuracy is sure to improve.)

- You stopped reading too soon. Maybe you got hung up on one feature without noticing other related traits. Remember, each feature has an interpretation of its own but also must be considered as part of the whole face.
- Lack of practice at using intuition. Rest assured, intuition may get stiff through neglect, but it won't atrophy. Where there's life, there are hunches.

   Maybe you've been told you're not a people person and ever since then have gotten by with using rules and formulas, plugging them in wherever they seem to fit.

   It might help to consciously check in with your feelings whenever you do this. Does the fit feel comfortable or not? Make adjustments to fit the situation you are in right now.
- A desire to show off, which cuts off the natural flow of intuition. Friend, you've got to leave your ego at the door if you want to walk into the hallway of intuition. Cultivate some childlike curiosity—it shrinks you to a size where you can wander at will through the teeny passageways of someone else's heart.
- A belief you know it all; the habit of judging people strictly as good or bad, with nothing in between; shyness; racism; or other attitudes that make it hard to look and listen deep.

What if none of these suggestions fits your particular case, but still you feel frustrated because your Readings are not getting the response you expect? Don't give up on your intuition—or Face Reading Secrets—as a lost cause.

When the student is ready, the teacher appears. So if you sincerely desire to develop clearer intuition, the best advice I can offer you is to keep on desiring. Sooner or later (often immediately) you'll attract the perfect teacher to take you a step farther.

THE FACE-READING LIFE-STYLE

If you read faces over a period of months or even weeks, wisdom about faces will become part of your life-style. Here are some long-term results my students have noticed:

- "I'm more observant about people. I remember their faces better. I can even remember their names better, now I have something to attach them to."
- "I use it a lot. Especially in business. My sales are going up."
- "My appreciation of people has grown by leaps and bounds."
- "Reading faces has made me less shy."
- "I've got to tell you, I enjoy using this stuff more than anything—and I'm a professional class-taker."

Just for fun you may want to turn to the Index of Facial Traits and browse through all the new traits you have learned to recognize.

You will be amazed at all you see now when you look at a face.

FIVE FAMOUS FACES

There are so many ways to use Face Reading Secrets. I approached each of the following close-up readings differently. For each famous face, you'll find the overall perspective summarized in a box.

THE MONA LISA
Ruthless Ambition

- Basic reading for personal style
- A customer service perspective

Revered for centuries as a symbol of beauty and mystery, this twenty-four-year-old Florentine housewife has earned quite a reputation for herself. But reading her face in the usual way won't tell you much about the flesh-and-blood person. What was she really like?

With Face Reading Secrets, you can interpret more accurately than the so-called experts.

Consider Walter Pater. When pondering the expression on Leonardo da Vinci's portrait, he envisaged "strange thoughts and fantastic reveries and exquisite passions."

With all respect to the great art critic, his reaction is a good example of just how misleading expression reading can be. Pater wasn't the first man to "read" a face by projecting his mood onto someone else.

And Mona Lisa was no dreamy-eyed babe.

A more contemporary critic, Kenneth Clark, has gotten closer to the truth: "The 'Mona Lisa' has been irreverently described as 'the cat that's eaten the canary': which expresses well enough the smile of one who has attained complete possession of what she loved, and is enjoying the process of absorption."

Right on! But let's look beyond expression, to see *what* kind of person she was and *why* she looked so satisfied.

DRAMATIC CONTRASTS

What strikes you first about Mona Lisa's face traits? To me, it's contrast. See how much physical space is taken up by her huge, broad cheeks and intensely long nose? This big facial statement gets punctuated by an amazingly tiny chin. Quite a contrast, isn't it?

Similarly, compare that immense forehead to the minuscule mouth.

These contrasts aren't just dramatic. They are highly significant.

RUTHLESS AMBITION

The dominant proportions of her nose (*Priority Area 2*) show that Mona Lisa was intensely ambitious. *Broad cheeks* accentuate this. Attention, influence, and personal power mattered more than anything else. You couldn't stand in her way for long.

Angled chin shape shows that she would make decisions without considering people or principles. She was driven by the need to stay in control. When combined with her passion for getting her way, that chin stands for ruthlessness.

Do you remember how *small chin* size goes with vulnerability to criticism? In her case, given the voracious appetite for power, Mona Lisa probably had a challenge with what we today call paranoia. I don't mean that she was crazy—just a bit queenlike. She didn't tolerate being scoffed at by her "subjects."

Is there a positive side? For starters, she's just the gal you'd want to marry if you wanted to be kinglike!

And whatever your ambitions, if you could get this woman to support you, she could be a wonderful ally. Since her husband, Francesco del Giocondo, isn't around to tell you about it, let me count the ways:

1. *Deep-set eyes*—ability to act polite, while secretly assessing everyone.
2. *Wariness*—on the scale from 1 to 10, Mona Lisa scores 2; about as wary as she could be. (Examine the shape of her lower eyelids to read wariness, and you will probably do a double take. Much straighter than you would expect, isn't it?) The practical advantage is this: If you can win her loyalty, you're set for life.
3. *Large eyelid area*—the generous rim of flesh over her eyelashes shows the capacity for closeness. Her husband would benefit from tender demonstrations of affection and genuine faithfulness.

4. *Nose length*—her talent for strategy might come in handy. Remember, she lived in the same culture that brought the world Machiavelli (the unabashed power broker who makes The Godfather look like the nice guy on the block).

HER CHALLENGE WITH POWER

The contrast between the large forehead and tiny mouth reveals Mona Lisa's challenge with power. We have already seen that she tends to be very aware of power . . . and skillful at getting it. The challenge lies in her ability to enjoy what she wins.

The *large forehead* suggests intellectualism. She thinks a great deal (in fact, this is part of her talent for strategy).

Yet the *tiny mouth* suggests that she expresses only a small fraction of what she has to say. Especially with those *puckers at the corners of her lips*, I wouldn't expect Mona Lisa to be especially good at speaking up for her feelings. Even in a close relationship, she would stay on her guard.

This lack of personal sharing, combined with the formidable ambition, tell me that Mona Lisa's power seeking was ultimately frustrating. Materially, she may have been adroit as a wheeler-dealer. Emotionally, she seldom had enough.

History brings us a revealing anecdote about how La Gioconda's portrait was made. Leonardo worked on it for three years. He made special arrangements to entertain her during the portrait sittings. Musicians and jesters performed, to keep her amused.

According to Vasari, who chronicled this in his *Lives of the Artists*, the purpose was to prevent her looking "melancholy" (i.e., bored) as a result of prolonged posing.

Nonsense! The multitalented da Vinci was a shrewd practitioner of what we today would call customer service. Here was a lady easily discontented, who demanded the royal treatment. He knew he'd *better* keep her amused.

In more ways than one, this painting is a tribute to La Gioconda's talent for power seeking. Had she lived in our day, she would have thrust her way to fame as a business-woman or politician. Yet, despite her limited options as a woman in Renaissance Italy, look at what she achieved.

Painted by one of the greatest artists who ever lived, she attained a kind of immortality.

ELVIS PRESLEY
How His Sexiness Changed

* Reading for sexiness
* Overcoming your dislike of someone by looking deeper
* Seeing physical and inner changes over time

Ask any Elvis fan. There are two kinds of people in the world. Some go wild over The King. Others are losers.

Admittedly, I'm one of the skeptics. I have wondered, why all the fuss about Elvis? Will there ever come a time I can stand in line at the supermarket, scanning the tabloids, without reading "Presley"?

Yet I believe that Face Reading Secrets can help one find a way in to appreciate anyone. So I'll use it to tackle a rock 'n' roll singer whose charms have always eluded me. Also, I'll use Elvis's example to illustrate how you can read anyone for sexiness—from movie stars to the guys and gals hanging out at your neighborhood bar.

Another technique I'll illustrate in this reading is using photos to read how someone changes over time. Photo A, shown here, was taken in 1960, when Elvis was twenty-five. Photo B dates from 1972, when he was thirty-seven.

Photo A

Photo B

EARTHIER AND EARTHIER

Always an earthy guy, Elvis actually grew more macho in one important respect. Look at the proportion of his three *Priority Areas*.

Hairline to eyebrows was always smallest. This proportion for Priority Area 1 always indicates a mistrust of intellectualism—which remained constant for Elvis over the years. (This contributed directness to his appeal.)

Eyebrows to nose tip was largest when Elvis started out as a deeply ambitious young singer. As you'll recall, a predominant Area 2 parallels inner drive to make a name for yourself . . . and get paid for your efforts.

But look at what happened to Area 3, from nose tip to the end of the chin. Domination as he aged! This suggests that physical experience grew in importance for Presley.

In a way, this is not surprising. He was making a career as a sex symbol and, in the words of one great proverb, *what you put your attention on gets stronger in your life.* Interestingly, though, Presley also happens to have *every* other major sign of an intensely physical orientation.

Consider his *large earlobes,* culminating in circular puffs of flesh. They mean that Presley tended to be unusually observant of physical reality—the shapes and movements of the bodies around him.

Presley's *overlip* area is also unusually well defined. A close-up view reveals two sharply etched parallel lines connecting nose and mouth. This relates to constant awareness of maleness versus femaleness. Most of us live in a far more unisex world than Elvis did.

The clincher though, for physical awareness, is the *circular knob* protruding at the end of his chin. You must look for this carefully, because it isn't as sharply etched as on more contemporary sex symbols Tom Selleck and Ted Danson.

The meaning, however, is the same: a macho pride in his masculinity. You don't call this kind of man a wimp and get away with it.

MORE ABOUT SEXUAL STYLE

Do all these traits guarantee that you will find Elvis sexy? No, because his very physical orientation may not match your life priorities. If your face shows a very large Area 1 or very small Area 3, chances are that you don't stay fascinated for long with a date whose face is dominated by Area 3.

This illustrates a key factor in reading someone's face for sexiness. Over the long term, for adults, compatibility matters more than purely physical attributes.

Sexiness involves personal style. The more you define sex as making love, the more important personal style becomes. Here are some other elements that relate to Elvis's style as a sexual communicator.

Unconscious emotional openness shows in Elvis's ears. Not only did his ears have *deep inner circles*. More unusual, they were marked with a *raised border*. This combination suggests an intense emotional life, which he had a talent for expressing without inhibition (Oprah Winfrey, who has similar raised borders, has used this uninhibitedness to turn her famous talk shows into marathons of emotional processing).

Conscious openness shows in the Wariness Index. This is one place where Elvis changed significantly over the years. At twenty-five, his lower eyelids scored 9 out of 10 points. He couldn't have been much more wide open. Twelve years later, he scored 4 on the right eye and 2 on the left. Emotionally, The King had closed down.

For fans, this toughness would only make Elvis more appealing, in the time-honored tradition of playing hard to get. So would the way his nose changed.

That's right, look carefully at the length of Elvis's nose from bridge to tip in both these pictures. Do you see how a *slender area* developed down the center? This suggests dramatically increased independence when he was working. Elvis had to do things his way—no compromises.

Elvis's style of expression made his loner style especially tantalizing. Obviously, his performances reveal him to be an unabashed communicator. To find out *why*, read his face.

Low brows mean that spontaneous expression worked best for Elvis. He wasn't the kind of man who liked to store up his feelings. Speak now, pay later was his motto.

Close-set cheeks developed over time. This reveals an increasingly powerful style, where he could blast out a great deal of energy, fast. (Short-distance runners aren't the only performers who need to sprint. Ask any professional musician.)

Finally, we come to the great Presley mouth. Fans will tell you, that never changed. The very curved, *full lower lip* suggested a let-it-all-hang-out style of self-expression.

The clearly *defined upper lip* revealed a talent for manifestation. Whether singing or speaking, Elvis had a gift for making his words come true.

Most important, the lip proportions show strong persuasive ability. Elvis is one of best examples you'll ever see of what I've referred to as Blarney Lips.

How did Elvis change? He began as a spunky kid with hidden vulnerability. In addition to the aforementioned openness, do you see the *third white showing under each eye* in Photo A? That denotes a pattern of feeling inferior.

As the performer grew in success, he gained confidence, power, and independence. His sexiness matured to an intense earthiness. Before he burned himself out at forty-two, he had served countless fans as a symbol of their own raw, vital passion.

BARBARA BUSH
A Friend Worth Having

> - Firsthand information about celebrities
> - Reading for friendship potential
> - Being surprised, even by a face you know well

What would Barbara Bush be like as a friend? Read her lips. Read her whole face and get to know her as well as if you lived next door to the White House.

FIRST IMPRESSIONS

From the first visit on, Barbara's manners would charm you. The *broad, curved chin* shows that she values hospitality. Moreover, her chin-to-nose area stacks up as the largest of her three *Priority Areas*. Thus, Barbara would check in with reality while visiting with you. She would ask questions, listen intently. Her down-to-earth perspective would help convince you of her genuine interest.

Barbara also would impress you with her high level of involvement while talking with you. The explanation lies in her eye set. Both eyes, and especially the right one, protrude somewhat. Granted, there are health reasons for this physical trait; but they don't explain it away any more than other excuses people may give for their physical traits.

So, on the level of Face Reading Secrets, Mrs. Bush's *protruding eyes* tell you she gets deeply enmeshed in conversation. As a friend, you would benefit.

AS A CLOSE FRIEND

Assuming you were able to establish a close friendship, you would especially value Barbara's compassion.

She's a people person. It shows in her *curved eyebrows* and *large inner ear circles*. Beyond this . . .

Look at those downward-sloping eye angles. Here's one lady who can handle talking about problems, whether helping you look for solutions or simply listening. Everyone should make at least one friend with *pessimist eyes*.

Frankness is a related strong point. Barbara would tell you honestly where you stood with her. And yes, you would have to ask before she told you. She has learned the trick of using those *outspoken lips* (in her smile, proportions of upper and lower lips are equal, the mark of outspokenness).

MONEY

The First Lady creates an overall image of hospitality and generosity with guests but probably cuts corners in accordance with her instincts for frugality. Her trademark fake pearls represent a way of life, not just a fashion idiosyncrasy.

Barbara's money style shows in her *substantial nose tip*, with *small nostrils*. Financial security dominates her economic agenda. Don't expect her to be big on mad money.

Look closely at Barbara's face and you'll notice that she has a way of smiling so big that her *gums show*. Read that as challenge over generosity issues. She may go frugal in some situations, overgiving in others—swing back and forth as she learns her own best way to set limits.

SEX

Barbara is comfortable with her sexiness, which includes an insistence on connecting emotionally as well as physically. This shows in the curved lower eyelids of the *Wariness Index*, the *curved chin*, and *curved eyebrows*.

She is physically demonstrative. Read that in her afore-mentioned *large grounding area*, from nose to chin. Also, Barbara's mouth in repose has thin lips, hinting at a chal-lenge with expressing deep personal feelings—and that's a challenge she shares with the man who said "Read my lips."

Combine the reticence with verbal self-disclosure along with the physicality and you get someone who shows affection rather than just talking about it.

This integration of sex, emotion, and behavior could help Barbara keep sex a vital part of a long marriage.

PARENTING

Barbara knows how to accept people for what they are, in-cluding young ones, so she can avoid trying to make children over in her own image. This shows in the aforementioned eye traits of openness and eye set.

Despite this kind of freedom, however, you'd expect her to be a strict parent. For instance, she gets very involved when talking, as we've seen in the discussion on eye set. The children's (and grandchildren's) training in manners would emphasize *no interrupting*.

Also, in questions of moral issues and personal values, Barbara expects to be considered "the authority." This shows in *high cheekbones*, markedly higher on the left side of her face. Children would learn in no uncertain terms what Bar-bara considers right and wrong.

THE BIGGEST SURPRISE

Mrs. Bush has all the instincts of an athlete: physical stamina; physical aggression; performs well under pressure. Just take a peek at those *powerful jaws, close-set cheeks* and *prominent chin*.

MAJOR LIFE LESSON

Caring independence shows in Barbara's traits for nonconformity of thought, need for creative control over work projects, and not depending on support from others. She is her own person.

You'll find confirmation in her *leaderlike, unpadded cheeks, downturned nose tip, low ear position,* and *eye angle*. And we've already seen other components of independence in eye set, Priority Areas, and cheeks.

The change in lip proportions when Barbara smiles is significant. Barbara's official smile puffs her lips out to a greater fullness, and changes lip proportions to equal. When not smiling, her lips are considerably thinner, and the upper lip nearly disappears.

So the public version of her independence is outspokenness; the private version is keeping silent. If it's deeply personal, Barbara will tell you when she's good and ready.

What do the public—and you—stand to gain from Barbara Bush's caring independence? She's a wonderful role model, because she gets deeply involved in people and their problems yet keeps her own boundaries firm.

The challenge that goes with it: Lack of personal flexibility is the biggest potential problem. Barbara doesn't jump to conclusions (especially with those *low ears*), but once she makes up her mind, that's it. Just because she gets deeply involved, she invests heavily in her beliefs. I wouldn't want to be the one to demand that Barbara Bush change her mind!

EDDIE MURPHY
Outrageous Vision

> • Reading for sales effectiveness
> • Finding out what makes someone special
> • Comparing sides of the face

Just for fun, my portrait of this intensely talented comedian will start with a salesperson's perspective. Among the five faces shown here, Murphy is the richest. If you were in the business of selling clothes or cars or castles, how would you persuade him to part with his money?

Here are the practical points to note for a sales pitch:

1. Nostrils first is the way to go, when you are selling a new prospect. Take your cue from the size and shape of the nostrils, read in combination with the nose tip.

   In Murphy, you'll be delighted to recognize *large nostrils with a rectangular shape*, plus a *moderate-sized nose tip*. That spells an emphasis on spending rather than saving. Translated into sales-ese, Murphy's nose means: emphasize the fun he'll have now, not potential economies of the future.

   The rectangular nostril shape could spell trouble in a different customer . . . a man in a different income-bracket. As you'll recall, rectangles can suggest relatively joyless spending, grim sticking to a budget. Fortunately, when there is more money to spend, the same trait goes with enjoyment of *hiding* how much money there is to spend from a spouse or a salesperson.

But don't let Eddie get away with pretending he doesn't want to buy. Each of the following five traits tells you that Murphy will greatly enjoy spending his money. For him, nostril size matters more than shape, and he's got an easy-spending size.

2. Appeal to his vision. The most *very* trait in Eddie Murphy's face are those wonderful *far-set eyes*. So don't narrow in on every minor feature of your merchandise. Make a broad appeal to his imagination.

3. Use emotional terms. With those intensely *curved eyebrows*, Murphy notices fine nuances of feeling.

   Say you're selling him a car. Appeal to his sensitivity by painting a picture of how he and his friends will feel zooming around in style. For heaven's sake, don't try to convince the man with dry facts like gas mileage.

4. *Face proportions* show that earthiness is a Life Priority, followed by ambition. Abstract conjecture won't appeal to him. Instead, give him a whack at hands-on experience. After you paint the grand vision of what your product can do, let him test-drive.

5. Nonconformity runs rampant in those *out-angled ears*. Never feed Murphy a line like "This is our most popular model." You'll do better with "This is our most unpopular model. . . . Aren't the others fools?"

6. The *long, full mouth* shows you right away about Murphy's style of self-expression. Even if, somehow, you didn't know his reputation, one look at that mouth would tell you he isn't shy.

Don't you be shy either. Speak up, and use superlatives to describe your product.

A COMEDIC WONDER

Letting the sales approach go, you can interpret the afore-mentioned traits in a different way. Most of us won't get to meet Eddie Murphy in person, let alone throw him a sales pitch. But we can read Eddie's face as the experienced (if unofficial) TV and movie critics we are.

DOOMED TO BE EXPRESSIVE?

Murphy's style of imagination shows in the upper half of the face (as it does for everyone), while the lower half tells you how that imagination will be expressed. For this comedian, the outrageous self-expression perfectly matches the outrageous imagination.

At the same time, with Murphy's down-to-earth priorities, big ideas are applied to the little things of life. Reality gets tested—and made to flunk.

As a communicator, Murphy has two special traits that accentuate his outrageous big mouth style.

First, his *mustache* is trimmed to keep the upper lip exposed. That's a good move because, as we've seen, that keeps it relatively easy for a mustache owner to express his personal reactions and feelings.

Second, check out Murphy's mouth in repose and you'll notice that rarest of *mouth angles*. He's an optimist. His challenge is too much rough joking, not knowing when to stop. The strength is his ability to handle criticism (accentuated by that generous chin).

Even if Eddie Murphy had chosen to be something other than a comedian, that wonderful optimist, mustache-free mouth ensures that he'd be a wild and crazy guy, uninhibited to the core.

DEEPER SECRETS

When you compare the different sides of Murphy's face, you gain a whole new level of insight into the complexity of Murphy's personality.

The first difference I'll note is that his *left eyebrow is higher* than the right. It angles more, too.

This suggests that the Murphy can be confrontational, even temperamental. Or he can come across as a smooth mover. He has extra flexibility. (He also has extra potential to give himself a hard time. No matter which way he acts, the other part of him can criticize.)

Difference in *eye angles* shows that he presents himself as a realist but feels like an optimist. Appearing a bit tougher than he actually is may serve as protection. The challenge aspect is that the combination of extremely far-set eyes, very curved brows, and even *one* optimist eye opens Eddie up to high ideals that could collapse on him, leading to bitter disappointment.

This challenge becomes accentuated in personal relationships. Compare the *eyelid thickness* on both sides of his face and you'll discover that Murphy's right eyelid is about 50 percent fuller than the left one. Part of him can get overly dependent, while the other part scoffs.

Finally, *the left ear angles out more* than the right. I suspect Murphy has a deep challenge with not feeling that he belongs. Personal relationships are always being tested. On the other hand, he benefits from understanding the range of conformity. He can sympathize with establishment types as well as social rebels because, inside, he experiences both styles.

Overall, Eddie Murphy's face is more symmetrical than most. So the way he comes across to others is not terribly different from how he feels.

Look carefully at the eyebrow area and you may notice *a*

muscular ridge stretching clear across the forehead. Do you see that bulge? It is the mark of inner denial, and can accompany a reluctance to see painful truths about oneself.

For Murphy, so far this is a slight challenge. The way he handles it is critical. If he came to me for a face-reading session, I'd make a strong recommendation about his personal life: Don't say things to impress people and risk speaking from the heart.

ALBERT EINSTEIN
A Passion for Truth

* Tuning in to genius
* Comparing views of left and right sides of the face
* Contrasting public and private sides of personality

Fortunately, you don't have to be able to understand a word of Einstein's theories of relativity to learn the secrets of his face.

UNUSUAL TRAITS MARK EXCEPTIONAL TALENTS

Three long, broken lines reach clear across from one side of the head to the other. Additional lines form just at the temple. "Just forehead wrinkles," a casual observer might think.

But hold on! Compare his forehead wrinkles to those of anyone else you know. Theirs may cover the center of the face, but do they reach all the way out to the ears? Not likely.

You've heard it rumored that Einstein used more of his mental potential than most of us. Here's the facial evidence.

Next, take a look at Einstein's right ear. See how the *top angles out*?

You'll recall that outer and inner ear circles symbolize awareness of objective and subjective experience. For Einstein, the outer, objective portion sticks out at an extreme angle. Read it as a talent for understanding objective reality.

Third, observe the right eyebrow. What shape would you say it is?

You might answer straight, curved, *or* angled. No matter which, I'd have to say you're correct. All these shapes can be seen. Einstein has what I call *chameleon* eyebrows. They take on all possible shapes. This parallels unusual mental flexibility.

And while we're gazing at his right brow, here's yet one more unusual trait not mentioned elsewhere in this book. Notice the height. *The eyebrow starts off lower at his nose and rises considerably.*

Whenever you find an eyebrow that rises like this, read it as ability to keep up with the future. Because Einstein's **leading edge brow** is on the right side only, the interpretation is that it shows in his work, not his personal life. I don't reduce his efforts of a lifetime to this one trait . . . but it did help him stay ahead of his fellow physicists.

INNER CONFLICTS

Other traits were more of a mixed blessing for the great physicist.

Where's his mouth? *Small and covered up by a huge mustache*, the mouth suggests a challenge with personal self-expression.

The *delicate chin*, like Mona Lisa's, reveals sensitivity to criticism. Reading in conjunction with their other face traits, I would add to the interpretation for him (not for her) the positive side of this trait—intensely strong ethical standards.

Einstein's intensely *rounded eyes* are one of the first things people usually notice about his picture. Of course, as an expert at Face Reading Secrets, the part of his eyes you'll especially notice are the lower eyelids.

For this Wariness Index, I assign Einstein 9 for the right eye, 7.5 for the left.

Remember, the scale runs from 1 to 10, with 10 the most open. Thus, Einstein's eyes proclaim a truly open mind, especially where work is concerned. The potential challenge here is vulnerability.

This gets accentuated by the third white showing slightly in both eyes, especially the right. So, ludicrous though it may seem, Einstein probably put other physicists on a pedestal, comparing his own work disparagingly to theirs.

Also, by the time this photo was taken, Einstein evidently had some chronic health problems. The aforementioned sampaku right eye (three whites showing) is one indicator. Another is the *slender left jaw*, denoting lack of physical stamina. In his work (symbolized by right jaw) he came across as more vigorous than he felt the rest of the time.

Einstein also had several *burnout lines*. These are the horizontal wrinkles across the bridge of his nose. If a man with lines like Einstein's came for a face reading, here's how I'd advise him:

"You have a tendency to work too hard. If you can balance your career with the rest of your life, you'll have more energy. Otherwise, be sure to schedule yourself times to catch up on rest. One way or another you'll have to ease up on yourself, whether it's a vacation or a collapse."

COMPARING RIGHT AND LEFT

Einstein's right side is the one that will go down in history: the forward thinking brow, the talent for objectivity that shows in his right ear, the openmindedness in the lower eyelid.

An additional trait, more pronounced on the right, is the *nose groove*. The line at the right tip of the nose proclaims fierce independence—reluctance to accept help or money from others—determination to "do it myself."

The *realist angle* of his right eye also furthers his objectivity and persistence as a scientist. (It's a persistence born of pragmatism. Compared to a more idealistic style of scientist, he's not as apt to get discouraged when discoveries make him throw away hypotheses.) His right side shows him to be a powerhouse. The dynamism and strength are almost overwhelming.

Contrast this with his left side, the portrait of Einstein's private self. Just on the level of expression, isn't this view revealing? To me, it portrays emotional struggle just as clearly as the right view pictures uncompromising passion for truth.

You may see it differently; that's the tricky aspect of reading for expression. The level of facial traits has the advantage of being much more specific.

The eye angles, for instance, are clearly different. The upward angled, *optimist left eye* reveals greater idealism . . . and with it the capacity for more bitter disappointment. More wariness in the left eye, shown by the straighter eyelid, suggests shyness, even inaccessibility on a personal level.

If you look closely at the wrinkles from nose to mouth, you'll observe that on the left side those wrinkles extend past the mouth, all the way to the chin.

That's significant because this line is the index of deep emotional pain. The longer and deeper the line from nose to mouth, the more the bearer has suffered—either personally or through empathy for others. (*Note:* conflict and other forms of unhappiness show in other ways, as discussed elsewhere in the book.)

I doubt you will ever see one of these "pain lines" longer than the one on Einstein's left side.

Altogether, this side reveals the sensitivity behind Einstein's uncompromising passion for truth. His was a life worth living—but hardly easy.

APPENDIX: QUICK CHECKLIST FOR FACE READING SECRETS

LOOK HERE FIRST

Facial Trait
[   ] Eyebrow thickness
[   ] Eyebrow shape
[   ] Ear position
[   ] Ear angle
[   ] Lower eyelid curve

Personal Style
Thinking patterns
Orientation
Decision speed
Conformity
Wariness Index

Facial Trait	Personal Style
[ ] Nose tip size	Saving
[ ] Nostril size and shape	Spending
[ ] Nose length and shape	Work talents
[ ] Cheek padding	Cooperation
[ ] Cheeks proportions	Leadership
[ ] Chin prominence	Aggression
[ ] Chin width	Endurance
[ ] Chin shape and size	Ethics
[ ] Mouth length and thickness	Self-expression
[ ] Teeth	Major decisions
[ ] Face proportions	Life priorities
[ ] Optimism Index	Action and acceptance

WATCH FOR THESE SPECIAL TRAITS

Eyebrows:

[ ] Contradictory hairs	Confusion or conflict
[ ] Scattered hairs	Focus scatters
[ ] Eyebrow roots show	Anticipates problems
[ ] Unibrow	Nonstop thinking
[ ] Brow height	Verbal spontaneity

Ears:

[ ] Ear circles	Subjective-objective balance

Eyes:

[ ] Eye protrusion	Reserve
[ ] Eye distance	Perspective
[ ] Eyelid thickness	Intimacy
[ ] Eyelash thickness, eye puffs	Temper

Noses:

[ ] Roots, groove	Family support
[ ] Padding	Work extraversion
[ ] Tip angle	Impetuousness

Jaws:
[   ] Width   Stamina, loyalty
Chin:
[   ] Broadness   Sexual survivor
[   ] Dimples, clefts   Playful decisions
[   ] Beard shape   Ethics
Mouth:
[   ] Lower lip proportion   Persuasive gifts
[   ] Upper lip proportion   Outspokenness
[   ] Cupid's bow   Materializer
[   ] Corner puckers   Fear of ridicule
Teeth:
[   ] Front   Egoism
[   ] Spacing   Life choices
[   ] Overbite or underbite   Flexibility

BIBLIOGRAPHY

While there have been other books published on face reading, the following titles are the books I think you'll find most helpful.

Face Reading

De Mente, Boye. *Face-reading for Fun and Profit.* Phoenix: Bachelor Books, 1968.

Mitchell, M. E. *How to Read the Language of the Face.* New York: Macmillan, 1968.

Young, Lailan. *Secrets of the Face.* Boston: Little, Brown, 1984.

Books of Related Interest

Bellak, Leopold, and Baker, Samm S. *Reading Faces.* New York: Holt, Rinehart and Winston, 1981.

Carter, Mildred. *Helping Yourself with Foot Reflexology.* West Nyack, N.Y.: Parker, 1969.

Carter, Mildred. *Hand Reflexology: Key to Perfect Health.* West Nyack, N.Y.: Parker, 1975.

Dychtwald, Ken. *Bodymind.* Los Angeles: J. P. Tarcher, 1968 (revised 1986).

Ekman, Paul. *Telling Lies.* New York: W. W. Norton, 1985.

Hay, Louise L. *Heal Your Body: The Mental Causes for Physical Illness and the Metaphysical Way to Overcome Them*. Santa Monica, Calif.: Hay House, 1982.

Hilarion. *Body Signs*. Queensville, Ont.: Marcus Books, 1982.

Kushi, Michio. *How to See Your Health: The Book of Oriental Diagnosis*. Tokyo: Japan Publications, 1980. (I don't recommend this book, but it does provide an interesting look at the diagnostic approach to reading faces.)

INDEX—
FAMOUS FACES

These people were chosen to represent as many walks of life as possible. Though all are famous, not all names will necessarily be familiar to you. Racing fans will recognize Steve Cauthen; history buffs, Rasputin. I hope there will be plenty of known faces for everyone.

Probably the most universally famous faces in America belong to performers on TV and in the movies. Unfortunately, the star's personal qualities may be quite different from the image on the screen or in the gossip columns. So I favored people known for other achievements.

In private life, celebrities are people, not their titles. In a philosophical sense, nobody on this earth is more important than anyone else. This belief is important to me, so I chose to be informal here. I only kept titles for people you'd never recognize without their given names, like Diana, Princess of Wales.

INDEX—
FACIAL TRAITS

If you'd like to learn more about Face Reading Secrets™ and how to get your face read through the mail, write to me at:

AHA! Experiences
P.O. Box 13046
Silver Spring, MD 20911-3046

Please remember to enclose a stamped, self-addressed #10 envelope (business size).

I'm looking forward to hearing from you.

Laura Rosetree